ILLUSTRATIONS

OF THE

ROCK-CUT TEMPLES

OF

INDIA

TEXT TO ACCOMPANY THE FOLIO

VOLUME OF PLATES

JAMES FERGUSSON, Esq.

GYAN

Published by

GYAN

Gyan Publishing House
5, Ansari Road
Daryaganj, New Delhi-110002
Phone: 011-47034999, 9811692060
E-mail: books@gyanbooks.com

Distribution Network
gyanbooks.com
India, USA, Canada, UK, Australia, France

ISBN : 978-81-212-9260-3 (PB)
First Published, 1845

2nd Impression 2023

Printed at: Gyan Press, Delhi.

ILLUSTRATIONS OF THE ROCK-CUT TEMPLES OF INDIA
Author: JAMES FERGUSSON

ILLUSTRATIONS

OF THE

ROCK-CUT TEMPLES

OF

INDIA

ILLUSTRATIONS

OF THE

ROCK-CUT TEMPLES

OF

INDIA.

TEXT TO ACCOMPANY THE FOLIO
VOLUME OF PLATES.

BY

JAMES FERGUSSON, Esq.

LONDON:
JOHN WEALE,
No. 59, HIGH HOLBORN.
1845.

Dedication.

TO THE

PRESIDENT AND FELLOWS

OF THE

ROYAL ASIATIC SOCIETY

OF

GREAT BRITAIN AND IRELAND,

THIS WORK

IS

RESPECTFULLY DEDICATED

BY THEIR

OBLIGED AND HUMBLE SERVANT

JAMES FERGUSSON.

PREFACE.

When the paper which forms the principal part of this volume was read to the Royal Asiatic Society, it was not my intention to publish illustrations of the Rock-cut Temples apart from the other buildings of the same age and style. I, at that time, proposed to bring out, in a series of about one hundred plates, a complete set of illustrations of the Buddhist, Hindoo, and Mahomedan styles, including not only those cut in the rock, but also the structural buildings, from the earliest date to the present day.

The difficulty, however, and trouble of bringing out such a work, and the certainty of a serious loss of money, consequent on the great expense of such works, and their limited sale in this country, deterred me from the attempt: and it was only from the interest expressed on the subject at the time, that I was induced to publish these plates as an experiment. Had it not been for this, the Rock-cut Temples are certainly not those I would have chosen for a first essay; for neither to the artist nor to the antiquary are they so interesting or so beautiful as the structural buildings of the same, or subsequent ages. They are, however, generally among the earliest examples of architecture in India, and may thus be considered as an appropriate commencement, should it afterwards be found expedient to continue the series.

At the same time it must be allowed that "the Caves" are almost the only object of antiquity in India, to which the learned in Europe have turned their attention, or of which travellers have thought it worth while to furnish descriptions, or whose history they have attempted to elucidate; and they therefore possess, to a European public, an interest which it would be difficult to excite for other works, without a more extended history of art in the East, than it would be worth while attempting till it could be ascertained whether the interest the public take in the subject would repay the author for his trouble.

The same reasons have deterred me from re-writing the essay which accompanies the plates, though I feel that it is not now in the form in which it ought to be presented to the general reader. When written it was merely intended to place on record, in the journal of a learned society, such observations as it appeared to me were new, or would be interesting to a body who had long before turned their attention to the subject. But as they had already in their Transactions, or in those of the sister Societies in India, several papers on the subject, I have, to avoid repeating what was already known to them, often passed over what would otherwise have been interesting to the general reader, and in like manner have as often dilated too much on what, to him, *must* appear of trivial importance, and throughout have assumed in my hearers more knowledge of the subject than I can expect the public to possess. When, however, I attempted the task of reconstruction, I found that

I must either write a volume on the subject, which would be absurd if the illustrations stop at these few plates, or if I attempted an abridgement of the present paper, I would merely render it useless to the enquirer, without making it more interesting to those who do not wish for more than a superficial knowledge of the subject. And as the Council of the Asiatic Society were kind enough to allow me to print the copies I required, from their types as they stood, I have preferred allowing it to stand as it is, though fully aware of its many imperfections, trusting that at some future period I may have an opportunity of affording the public fuller information on the subject, and in a more satisfactory form, than the present essay can pretend to.

INTRODUCTION.

DESCRIPTION OF THE PLATES.

VIGNETTE ON TITLE PAGE

Is a view of the Khandagiri hill at Cuttack, which is only separated by a narrow ravine from the Udyagiri hill, on which the principal Buddhist caves are situated. The principal cave, in the centre of the view, is the Jaina one mentioned page 13 as the largest on this hill; several others are seen on various parts of it, but the greater number are hid by the brushwood and trees. On the top of the hill is seen the Jaina temple, built by the Maharattas.

PLATE I.

The upper view is one of the two-storied caves of which several exist here, but in the present instance the upper story does not appear ever to have possessed a verandah, though protected by the projecting ledge of rock, and the doors open directly to the cells; as will be observed, however, they are built up by the Fakeers, who now inhabit them, and are very unwilling to admit strangers to examine their dark abodes.

The lower view represents the interior of the verandah of the Gunesa Gumpha*, with the doors leading to the cell. The two may be considered as fair average specimens, both as to size and style, of the generality of the old Buddhist caves in Cuttack.

* The sketch, plan of the cave Plate No. 1., contains an unpardonable mistake, inasmuch as there were originally five pillars in front of the verandah, but the one next the spectator having fallen away, it should be omitted. The remaining four have been placed equidistant, which of course they should not be.

PLATE II.

A general view of the latest caves at Ajunta, showing their position and size relatively to the rock in which they are cut; in which respect these caves have a decided advantage over all others I am acquainted with, and on the plate they appear of even more importance than in reality. They are also those situated highest in the rock. The series of caves slopes, on the right hand of the drawing, almost to the bed of the stream.

PLATE III.

Page 17.

The oldest Chaitya cave at Ajunta, and, excepting perhaps the one at Karli, perhaps in India. The wood work of the roof has entirely disappeared, leaving only the marks on the plaster where it has been, but the stone ribbing in the side aisles shows its form and disposition.

It is difficult to understand how the broad belt over the pillars has been ornamented, as no trace of plaster remains on it, though it is still tolerably entire both in the pillars below, and roof above this part: so that it probably was either covered with tapestry or wood work, as probably also was the dagopa, which shows the same denuded, unfinished appearance, except the tee on the summit.

PLATES IV. AND V.,

Page 19,

Represent the interiors of the two finest Vihara or monastery caves at Ajunta, Nos. 16 and 17. The first view is taken from the doorway, the second within the first colonnade, immediately behind the pillar represented in Plate 6 of this volume, in both instances looking inwards towards the sanctuary. Taken together they may serve to give a very tolerable idea of the architecture of these two beautiful caves, but my drawings were not sufficiently detailed to admit of my attempting to do justice to the frescoes, which owing to the imperfection of the light cannot easily be sketched from the same spot, but must have been drawn separately and afterwards transferred to the drawing; the position of one, however, is seen in the left-hand corner of Plate V., as distinctly as the light would allow me to draw it with the camera lucida.

PLATES VI. AND VII.,
Page 21, AND PLAN 3,

Taken together, will, I trust, serve to illustrate the form and disposition of one of the most perfect, though far from being one of the most splendid, Chaitya caves in India: in this instance every detail is cut in the solid rock, and there does not appear to have been a single wooden ornament on any part, either external or internal, so that we now see the cave nearly as it was left when first excavated. The dagopa in particular is the most perfect I know of, and the only one that has the tee with the three umbrellas in stone*; and enables us to supply several deficiencies not only in other caves, but in the great structural dagopas, which generally are shorn of this appendage, which however existed in all, and is the origin of the three and nine-storied towers of China, as I shall show elsewhere.

PLATE VIII.
Page 21.

An exterior view of cave No. 7. Externally one of the most elegant Viharas at Ajunta; it has, however, no internal hall, in which respect it differs considerably from most of those in this place, and looks more like the Brahmanical caves at Ellora, than a Buddhist Vihara. Its architecture is interesting; as the pillars have the same cushion capitals as are found at Elephanta, at Ellora (see Plate IX. of this vol.), at Salsette (see Plate XVI. of folio volume), and though something like them is found in the buildings of the south of India, nothing of the sort exists, that I am aware of, in any structural building to the north of the Nerbudda.

PLATE IX.
Page 23. PLAN 2,

Represents the verandah of one of the most modern caves at Ajunta, and compared with the verandah, Plate I., offers a comparison between one of the oldest and one of the most modern specimens of Buddhist cave architecture in India; the comparison however is scarcely fair to the Cuttack example, which is small and without much pretension, while this belongs to a cave of considerable pretension and richness; and lithographed by an artist who was not acquainted with the minute peculiarities of style, the

* Above the tee a cross is represented on the roof, which is not, however, a symbolical cross, as it at first sight appears, but merely a part of the construction at the junction of the lateral ribs with the centre one; but not being understood, it has been made too prominent by the artist, and was not perceived till too late to alter.

modern example looks better than it should do in comparison with the ancient one, which has scarcely had like justice done to it.

PLATE X.

Page 27.

An exterior view of the great cave at Karli, whieh I have described so fully in the text, that I need not repeat the description here. It is the only view in this volume that is not copied from a sketch of my own, made with the camera lucida, and I cannot therefore quite answer for the correctness of the proportion; but Mr. Salt's large plate, from which it is taken, is so unusually correct, as to supply all the details that are required for comparison. When at Karli I had this view in my possession, and finding it so perfect, I contented myself with making a few notes and corrections, as, owing to the great crowd at the fair, and the noise and confusion, it would have been by no means an easy task to make a detailed drawing myself. The cave is, however, so essential to the elucidation of the subject, that I have not hesitated to introduce it here, and with the annexed wood cut* of

* As I mentioned in the text, I have never personally visited the Behar cave, and the annexed cut is taken from a drawing in the Buchanan collection at the India House, collated with one in the Mackenzie collection at the same place, and is, I believe, tolerably correct.

the Lomas Rishi cave in Behar, will, I trust, throw some new light on the subject, as taken together I think they prove most distinctly the *wooden* origin of almost every member of this singular architecture; and if I am correct in conjecturing the Behar example (in spite of its inscription) to be the earliest façade of the sort, we see how little the first copiers deviated from their original, as every part of it is merely a repetition, in stone, of the wooden edifices attached to the great dagopas in Siam* and Burmah at the present day, making allowance for the difference of detail, arising from the different age and different country in which they are executed.

Karli is a step in advance of this, several parts being evidently either copied from masonry, or adapted to the material in which it was executed; and in subsequent examples, such as that shown Plate VI., the wooden origin is still further departed from; and as in the Vishwacarma at Ellora, all the parts which retain the wooden form are repeated in stone. In this early example at Karli, however, the framing in the great arch, the ribs of the roof, and the galleries on the screen were all in wood, and many parts of them still remain.

PLATES XI. AND XII.,

Page 36,

AND SMALL PLATE VIII. of this Volume.

The exterior view of the great Chaitya cave at Kannari, does not present the same means of comparison as that of Karli, for as all the ornaments of its front were in wood, and not one architectural detail executed in the rock, we have only the form of the coring by which to judge of their similarity. Plate XI., however, representing three pillars in each cave, furnishes more certain means of comparing the one with the other, and shows clearly the inferiority of design and execution displayed in the latter I insisted on in the text, and which induced me to assert that one was merely a bad copy of the other; an opinion I have since seen no reason to retract. These three plates, with the sketch, plan and section at the end of this volume, will, I trust, render the plan and design of these two caves as distinct as the nature of this work will admit of.

PLATES XIII. AND XIV.

Pages 38, 39.

The first of these is the Durbar cave, which though the finest Vihara at Kannari, is low in the principal story, and poor in its decoration, when

* CRAWFURD's *Embassy to Siam*, p. 110.

compared with the great examples at Ajunta and elsewhere. The second is a small Vihara higher up on the hill, and interesting as a type of all that series, and also as a means of comparison with those at Ajunta, Elephanta, and elsewhere, as I mentioned when describing Plate VIII., when alluding to those possessing the cushion-shaped capitals.

PLATE XV.

Page 49.

As the caves of Ellora have been so often drawn, this and the following are the only examples of this interesting series I have thought it necessary to introduce in these Illustrations. As the present view was carefully taken with the camera lucida, it will I believe be found more correct than any hitherto published, and it is so interesting an example, that the illustrations would not be complete without it, though its whole interest cannot be appreciated without the contemporary examples from the north and south of India, being placed in juxtaposition with it, so as to show the difference of style from those around it, as well as its striking similarity with the great temples of the Carnatic.

PLATE XVI.

Page 53.

I have introduced this plate not only that I might include a specimen of a Hindoo cave, but because it has been singularly overlooked by those who have published illustrations of Ellora, though its architecture is as fine as that of any similar cave of the series.

The difference between this example and a Buddhist Vihara, will be seen in the pillars standing all over the floor*, at equidistant, or at least similar, distances from one another, not round a hall as in the others; in their being almost all dissimilar, and in the details being boldly sculptured, and not trusting to painting for their decoration, as at Ajunta, besides the other peculiarities mentioned in the text†.

PLATE XVII.,

Page 56,

Will serve as a type of all the excavated caves at Mahavellipore. The leanness of the pillars shows how completely the spirit of cave architecture

* See Plan No. 4.

† There is an error in this plate in the floor on the right hand being cut back to the principal pillars, instead of extending to the outer range; it arose from my having accidentally rubbed out the line, in drawing the part of the Kylas seen in the view, and the artist having followed me too literally.

had degenerated into a copy of structural buildings, and the addition of the structural vimana on the top of the rock, adds another incongruity to its appearance; its pillars, however, show that remnant of the Elephanta cushion-form, which is still found in the Carnatic. It is altogether, however, an interesting example of the decline of the style which these plates are meant to illustrate.

PLATE XVIII.

Page 57.

The celebrated five Raths, each of which is sculptured out of a single block of granite protruding from the sand on the sea shore. In style they belong entirely to the southern type, and it will be observed that they (the second and last particularly) present many points of similarity with the Kylas at Ellora; to be aware, however, of the value of this comparison I should be able to prove the dissimilarity from other buildings, of which unfortunately, this series affords no examples.

The view is taken looking towards the sea, from which the full moon is rising, while the setting sun still tinges the buildings.

ON THE

ROCK-CUT TEMPLES OF INDIA.

THERE are few objects of antiquarian research that have attracted more attention from the learned in Europe, than the history and purposes of the Cave Temples of India, but if we except the still unexplained antiquities of Mexico, I know none regarding which so little that is satisfactory has been elicited, or about which so many, and such discordant opinions exist: and while the age of every building of Greece and Rome is known with the utmost precision, and the dates of even the Egyptian monuments ascertained with almost as much certainty as those of mediæval cathedrals, still all in India is darkness and uncertainty, and there is scarcely a work on architecture published, or lecture read, which does not commence by a comparison between the styles of India and Egypt, and after pointing out a similarity which seems to be an established point of faith in Europe, though in reality no two styles are more discordant, the author generally proceeds to doubt which is the more ancient of the two, and in most cases ascribes the palm of antiquity to the Indian as the prototype. Yet, in truth, Egypt had ceased to be a Nation before the earliest of the cave temples was excavated, and if we except the copies of earlier structures erected by the Ptolemies and Cæsars, there is nothing on the banks of the Nile which does not belong to a different and far more ancient epoch than anything in India.

Had Mr. James Prinsep lived to continue for a few years longer the researches which he commenced, and continued with such success, he probably would have succeeded in raising the veil which still shrouds in obscurity the antiquities of India; and though he has done much, and perhaps more than any one who preceded him, he was called away before his work was complete, and no one in India has since attempted to follow up the task he had proposed to himself. The spirit and enthusiasm he infused into all around him has died with him, and the subject of Indian antiquities relapsed into the former state of hopeless neglect.

The only attempt I am aware of to do any thing to follow up Mr. Prinsep's discoveries is that of Dr. Bird, of Bombay, who, while the spirit was strong in India, commenced the task of copying all the inscriptions in the cave temples on his side of India, and getting drawings made by some Portuguese assistants he had, of their architecture. When I was in Bombay in 1839, his work was in the press, and believing that it would soon be published, and that his testimony on the subject would be more valuable than mine, and probably sufficient to satisfy curiosity, I abandoned the idea of publishing my views on the subject; but when I revisited Bombay in the spring of the present year I found the work still in the press, and with apparently about the same chance of its being published now, as there was four years ago. I have been therefore induced to put the following remarks on paper, believing the subject to be one that could scarcely fail to be of interest to the Society. And I do this not with any idea of anticipating or forestalling Dr. Bird's work to which I would willingly give precedence if I saw any chance of its being published; but, because, as I believe our modes of research to have been totally different, the one may throw light on the other, and if I am not mistaken in what he told me of his work, they cannot interfere. *His* conclusions are drawn principally from the inscriptions and written authorities, while mine have been arrived at almost entirely from a critical survey of the whole series, and a careful comparison of one cave with another, and with the different structural buildings in their neighbourhood, the dates of which are, at least approximatively known. A combination of both these methods of research is necessary to settle any point definitely; but the inscriptions will not certainly by themselves answer that purpose, for in many instances they were cut long subsequent to the ascertained date of the cave, as in the Ganesa Gumpha[1], at Cuttack; and I have also reason to suspect, that, in some instances at least, the Buddhists affected an older character as more sacred, as we sometimes use old English letters in modern inscriptions. Unless, therefore, they contain names that can be identified in some of the lists we possess, or dates, the inferences they lead to, cannot in all cases be relied upon; and except the Behar caves I am not aware of any, where the names have been at all satisfactorily identified; and I do not know of any single cave inscription bearing a date from an ascertained era. Still the inscriptions form a most essential part of the inquiry, but one that I had neither leisure nor learning sufficient to devote myself to; and though I must consequently admit the imperfection of my labours from this cause, I had other advantages for prosecuting the inquiry that have fallen to the lot of few; for in the various journeys I undertook I was enabled to visit almost all the rock-cut Temples of India, from

[1] Gumpha, is the local designation for a cave at Cuttack; gurbha or garbha, would I believe be more correct.

those of Cuttack and Mahavellipore[1] on the east coast, to those of Ellora and Salsette on the western side; and there are few buildings or cities of importance in India which I have not at one time or other been able to visit and examine. I had besides the advantage, that as all my journies were undertaken for the sole purpose of antiquarian research, I was enabled to devote my whole and undivided attention to the subject, and all my notes and sketches were made with only one object in view, that of ascertaining the age and object of these hitherto mysterious structures. Whereas, most of those who have hitherto written on the subject, though drawing and writing better than I can pretend to do, have only visited the caves and temples incidentally while travelling on other avocations; and none that I know of, have been able to embrace so extensive a field of research as I have.

I hope, therefore, it will be understood, that the following remarks are not offered as the result of much learning or deep research, but simply as the practical experience of an architect in a favorite branch of his study.

In a short paper as the present is intended to be, it will be impossible to enter into all the arguments that may be urged for and against the various disputed points of Indian and Buddhist chronology; and though I am aware that I may often appear dogmatical in stating my conclusions, without adducing the reasoning from which they have been arrived at, I do not think I can be too concise, at least, in the first instance, and if any point appears to be of sufficient interest to the Society, I can afterwards add more detail than my limits at present admit of. I shall at the same time try to avoid, as much as possible, all hypothetical matter, and state merely what bears directly on the subject under consideration, and that as succinctly as possible; and I shall be less tempted to digress, as I have for some time past intended publishing a series of views, illustrative of this subject, accompanied by a volume of letter-press, in which I shall have abundant opportunity of stating all these views at length. That I may, however, be understood in the following remarks, I will state here the principal

[1] There are various ways of spelling and pronouncing the name of this place. The most popular, and the one by which it is generally known in Europe, is Mahabalipooram, "The city of the great Bali;" but which is now generally allowed to be incorrect, though adopted with a slight variation of spelling by Messrs. Chamber and Goldingham. Mr. Babington calls it Mahamalaipur, "The city of the great mountain," having found it so called in a Tamul inscription there.

Locally, it is called Mahavellipore, Maveliveram, Mailurum, &c. I have throughout this paper adopted the first, as most resembling its popular name, without pretending to any etymological correctness, or to any hypothesis regarding its origin or history.

conclusions I have arrived at regarding the religion of India, without entering on the grounds on which they were formed, or the reasoning by which they are supported.

The first is, That prior to the advent of the present Buddha, a Brahmanical religion existed in the country, a deistical fire-worship, very unlike the present religion bearing that name. That contemporary with this a Buddhistical religion also existed, differing but little from the other, probably two forms of the same religion. The former has entirely perished, and Buddhism, as we now know it, owes its origin to Gotama Buddha, the son of Suddodana; and was either an entirely new form given to the pre-existing religions, or what is more probable, a reform of both, meant probably to amalgamate the two. It could not however have differed much from the Brahmanism of those days, as we find the kings and people changing backwards and forwards, from one to the other, without difficulty or excitement; and in the description of the Greeks and in native records, we often find it difficult to distinguish between the one and the other.

2nd. It appears also certain that the correct date for Sakya Buddha obtaining Nirvana was 543 B.C. The principal authority opposed to this date are the trans-Himalayan chronologies, which generally concur in placing him about five hundred years earlier. They, however, contain their own refutation, (though I have never observed it pointed out,) inasmuch as they all place the event in the reign of Ajatasatta, and place Asoka little more than one hundred years after. Whereas, the date of the latter is perfectly ascertained to be about 250 B.C.; and of the former, not many years from when the Ceylonese authorities place it.

3rd. That from the time of Asoka till the destruction of the Andhra dynasty of Magadha in the beginning of the fifth century, Buddhism was the principal religion in the north of India, though in the south it never seems to have obtained a permanent footing, where the Brahmanical religion still prevailed, and during the time of Buddhist supremacy in the north, that form of it was elaborated which flowing back on the parent country exists in the form we now find it.

With regard to the antiquity of the monuments, all that is here necessary to state is, that the oldest relics of whose existence I am aware are the Laths, bearing the inscriptions of Asoka, dating from the middle of the third century B.C. I am not aware of the existence of any cave anterior to, or even coeval with these, nor of any structural building whose date can reach so high as the first centuries of our era.

I may also state that it appears quite evident that the Buddhists were the earliest cave diggers, and that it is not difficult to trace the connection of the whole series from "the earliest abode of Bauddha ascetics" at Nagarjuni, to the Kylas at Ellora; but as the principal object of the present paper is to point out this connection, I will not enlarge upon it more in this place; but in order to be understood, I must, before proceeding to describe particular caves, say a few words on the subject generally, to point out the different classes into which they are divided, and consequently, explain the names I shall apply to them throughout.

As far as my knowledge of the cave temples of India extends, the whole may be classified under the following heads.

First, Vihara, or Monastery Caves.

1st, The first subdivision of this class consists of natural caverns or caves slightly improved by art; they are as might be assumed the most ancient, and are only found appropriated to religious purposes in the older series of Behar and Cuttack; and though some are found among the western caves, their existence there appears to be quite accidental.

The second subdivision consists of a verandah, opening behind into cells for the abode of the priests, but without sanctuaries or images of any sort. The simplest form of this class consists of merely one square cell with a porch, several instances of which occur in the Cuttack series; sometimes the cell is nearly thirty feet long, as in the Ganesa Gumpha, of which a plan is herewith[1]; and at Ajunta in the oldest Vihara there, the arrangement is further extended by the verandah opening into a square hall, on three sides of which the cells are situated.

In the third subdivision of the Vihara caves, the last arrangement is further extended by the enlargement of the hall, and the consequent necessity of its centre being supported by pillars; and in this division besides the cells that surround the hall, there is always a deep recess facing the entrance, in which is generally placed a statue of Buddha with his usual attendants, thus fitting the cave to become not only an abode for the priests, but also a place of worship[2]. At Baug, the statue of Buddha is replaced by the Daghopa; but this is I believe a solitary instance of its existence in a Vihara cave.

To this division belongs by far the greatest number of Buddhist excavations. The most splendid of them are those at Ajunta; though the Dherwarra, at Ellora, is also fine; and there are also some good specimens at Salsette, and I believe Junir.

[1] Plate No. 1. [2] Plate No. 2.

The Second class consists of Buddhist Chaitya Caves[1].

These are the temples, or if I may use the expression, the churches of the series, and one or more of them is attached to every set of caves in the west of India, though none exist in the eastern side.

Unlike the Viharas, the plan and arrangement of all these caves is exactly the same; and though the details and sculpture vary with the age in which they were executed, some strong religious feeling seems to have attached the Buddhists to one particular form for their places of worship.

In the Viharas, we can trace the progress from the simple cavern to the perfect monastery, but these seem at once to have sprung to perfection, and the Karli cave, which is the most perfect, is, I believe, also the oldest in India. Had the style been gradually elaborated in the rock, from the imperishable nature of such monuments we could not fail to have discovered the earlier attempts; but besides this, there are many reasons that I shall notice in the proper place, which lead me to suppose that they are copies of the interior of structural buildings; and it is not one of the least singular circumstances attached to their history, that no trace of such buildings exists in India, nor, I believe, in Ceylon, nor in the Buddhist countries beyond the Ganges.

All these caves consist of an external porch, or music gallery, an internal gallery over the entrance, a centre aisle which I will call the nave, (from its resemblance to what bears that name in our churches,) which is always at least twice the length of its breadth, and is roofed a plain waggon vault; to this is added, a semi-dome terminating nave, under the centre of which always stands a Daghopa or haitya.

A narrow aisle always surrounds the whole interior, separated from the nave by a range of massive columns. The aisle is generally flat-roofed, though sometimes in the earlier examples it is covered by a semi-vault.

In the oldest temples the Daghopa consists of a plain circular drum, surmounted by a hemispherical dome crowned by a Tee, which supported the umbrella of state. In the earlier examples this was in wood, and as a general rule it may be asserted, that in these all the parts that would be constructed in wood in a structural building, are in wood in the caves; but in the more modern caves all those parts, such as the music gallery outside, the ribs of the roof, the ornaments of the Daghopa, the umbrella of state, &c., are repeated in the rock, though the same forms are preserved. In front of the more modern

[1] Plate No. 3.

Daghopas there is always a sculptural niche containing a figure of Buddha with his attendants; this may have existed in wood in the more ancient, and consequently have disappeared, but I am rather inclined to think it is a modern innovation.

These two classes comprehend all the Buddhist caves in India.

The Third class consists of Brahmanical *caves*, properly so called[1].

In form many of them are copies of, and all a good deal resemble the Buddhist Vihara, so much so as at first sight to lead to the supposition that they are appropriations of Buddhist caves to Brahmanical purposes. On a more intimate acquaintance however with them, many points of distinction are observed. The arrangement of the pillars, and the position of the sanctuary, is in no instance the same as in a Vihara; they are never surrounded by cells, as all Viharas are, and their walls are invariably covered, or meant to be, with sculpture; while the Viharas are almost as invariably decorated by painting, except the sanctuary. The subjects of the sculpture of course always set the question at rest.

The finest specimens of this class are at Ellora and Elephanta, though some good ones exist also on the Island of Salsette, and at Mahavellipore.

The Fourth class consists of rock-cut Models of structural Brahmanical temples, or, as I will call them, "Pseudo-structural temples." To this class belong the far-famed Kylas at Ellora, the Sivite temple at Doomnar, and the Ruths at Mahavellipore. Except the last, which are cut out of isolated blocks of granite, these temples possess the irremediable defects of standing in pits, which prevents them being properly seen, and the side of which being of course higher than the temples, crushes them and gives them an insignificant appearance; and though they are not the least interesting, they are in worse taste and worse grammar than any of the preceding ones.

The Indra Subha group at Ellora should perhaps form a Fifth class, as it cannot in strictness be brought under any of the above heads; but it is difficult to decide whether they are Brahmanical or Jaina; if the former, they belong to the third class, if the latter, they must be classed with what in reality form the

Fifth class, or true Jaina caves, which, without this splendid auxiliary are few and insignificant, though there are some tolerable ones at Khandagiri in Cuttack, and in the southern parts of India; and in the

[1] Plate No. 4.

rock of the fort at Gualior, there are a number of colossal figures of one or the other of the Thirthankars cut in the rock, with sometimes, though not always, a small screen left before them, which thus forms a small chamber. Some of them are sitting, some standing, and many of colossal dimensions, from thirty to forty feet high; the whole however is of rude bad sculpture, and the date about, or rather subsequent to the eleventh or twelfth century of the Christian era.

Before proceeding to describe particular caves, I may also mention here, that in speaking of Buddhist Chaitya caves, I have used terms borrowed from the names given by antiquarians to the different parts of Christian churches, because in form and arrangement they so exactly resemble the choirs, more particularly of the Norman churches of the eleventh and twelfth centuries, that no confusion can arise from my doing so, and I know not where to look for other terms, that would apply to them, and be intelligible.

In speaking of Hindu temples, as Ram Raz[1] is the only person who has attempted to describe and define the different parts of Hindu architecture, I have used his name, Vimana, to describe the principal tower, or pyramid, or spire, that surmounts the Garbhagriha, or sanctuary, in which the idol or object of worship is placed. In Hindustan, it is usually called Dewal, or Bara, or Bura Dewal, to distinguish it from the former, which is commonly applied to the whole temple. The pyramidal part is called Sikra or Surra, more commonly the former.

The porch which always stands in front of the Vimana, I have also followed Ram Raz in calling Mantapa, though locally it is called Bogha Mandap, Munduf, Muntapum, &c.

Other names of less frequent occurrence will be explained, if necessary, as they occur.

The first series of caves I will mention are those in Behar, which I have not myself seen, as from the descriptions I had read of them I knew that they possessed no great architectural magnificence, and I was not aware, till too late, that these were perhaps some of the oldest caves in India; and their locality, too, in the very birth-place of Buddhism, gives them an interest which no other series possesses, and which certainly would have led me to visit them, had I been as fully aware of it then, as I have since become; for situated in the immediate neighbourhood of Rajagriha, the capital of India at the time of Buddha's death, and where the first convocation was held, and in the neighbourhood of the capital of Asoka[2], they occupy the locality from which

1 Essay on the Architecture of the Hindús, 4to. London, 1834.

2 Mahawanso, pp. 22 and 23.

we might expect more of interest than from any series in India. To the artist, however, they are the least so of any, and were it not for the inscriptions on the Milkmaid's and other caves would be almost equally uninteresting to the antiquary. The cause of this I believe exists, to a certain extent, in the unfavourable nature of the rock in which they are cut, being a long low hill, consisting of large blocks of granite without any continuous rock. But more is, I am inclined to think, owing to these being the first attempts at cave architecture, and to the simplicity which is a distinguishing characteristic of all the earlier caves. It is in the northern arm of this hill that are situated two small vaulted caves, the first ten feet wide by fifteen long, and nine feet high, and the other about the same dimensions. In the inside they are partially polished, but without any architectural mouldings on them. It is on these caves that were found the two inscriptions in the Lath character, deciphered by Mr. Prinsep, in the sixth volume of the Journal of the Asiatic Society of Bengal, as follows:—

"The Brahman girl's cave (and the Milkmaid cave respectively), excavated by the hands of the most devoted sect of Bauddha ascetics for the purpose of a secluded residence, was appointed their habitation in perpetuity by Dasaratha, the beloved of the gods, immediately on his ascending the throne."

The character in which these inscriptions are written, evidently points to an era not distant from Asoka, and if the prince there mentioned is the Dasaratha, the grandson of that king, which I see no reason to doubt his being, we have at least two caves with an ascertained date, viz., about 200 B.C., and with the purpose for which they excavated explained.

As far as our researches have yet gone these are the most ancient caves in India; and I know of no other caves which from their locality, their form, or their inscriptions, can compete with them in this respect.

The other caves of this series are situated at some little distance from the above in the southern arm of the same hill, and though of greater extent, are generally as devoid of architectural ornament as those above described. It is therefore only to their inscriptions that we can look for materials to ascertain their dates or uses.

They consist of the Nagarjuni and Heft Kaneh, or Satghur group.

They have been described, first by Harington, in the first volume of the Asiatic Researches, and by Hamilton, in his Statistics of Behar.

The first contains the inscription first deciphered by Mr. Wilkins, and published with Mr. Harington's description, and which was revised by Mr. Prinsep in August, 1837.

After an invocation to Devi, it contains an inflated account of the virtues and great qualities of the king Yajna Verma, his son Sardula Verma, and his grandson Ananta Verma, who consecrated to this goddess (Devi) the beautiful village of Davidi, and it appears to have been to record this gift that the inscription was engraved.

The inscription on the Heft Kaneh is in the same character, and refers to the same parties.

The alphabet in which these inscriptions are written is very similar to that of the Gupta inscriptions, on the Allahabad Lath; if anything, more resembling the ancient Lath character; we could not therefore have much difficulty in fixing as their approximating date, the fifth century after Christ, and I do not think there can be much difficulty in identifying the Yajna Verma of the inscription, with the Yajna Sri of the Andhra dynasty of the Puranas, and who it is now generally allowed ascended the throne of Magadha, about the year 408 of our era.

The invocation to Devi and the language of the inscriptions is decidedly much more Brahmanical than Buddhist, and as they do not refer to the caves, we are left in uncertainty as to whether the Vermas really excavated them, and to what religion they were dedicated. It is difficult, however, to believe that any work of the Brahmans could be left without any indication of their polytheism, and the simplicity of the caves is a strong evidence in favour of their Buddhistical origin; and as there appears nothing to make us believe that the inscription is necessarily integral, but may have been added afterwards, it affords, I fear, no sufficient data for coming to any satisfactory conclusion regarding the monument in question.

A little further on is another group, the Karna Chapura, and the Lomas rishi caves. They appear to be adorned with some rude sculpture of a Brahmanical tendency. But none of the inscriptions on them that have been deciphered throw any light on their date, further than that they appear to be more modern than the two last referred to. But the drawings I have seen of their sculpture are much too imperfect and rude, to enable me to judge of their age by comparing them with the temples I have visited.

The next series in antiquity, and one of the most interesting in India, though one of the least known, are the caves of Khandagiri, situated about twenty miles from Cuttack, and five from Bobaneswar. There are here two small but picturesque and well-wooded hills of a coarse-grained sandstone, very rare in that neighbourhood, which seem from a very early period to have been a spot held particularly sacred by the Buddhists; and though no caves exist here that can vie in size or magnificence with those of Western India, there are a greater number of authentically ancient caves here, than in any other series, and the details of their architecture are of a higher class than any other I am acquainted with.

These caves were first described by Stirling, in his valuable Memoir on Cuttack, in the sixteenth volume of the Asiatic Researches, and drawings of some of them were published by Lieut. Kittoe, in the sixth and seventh volumes of the Journal of the Asiatic Society; they still however require and deserve a much more careful examination than either of those gentlemen have been able to bestow on them, though the task is by no means an easy one, for they are still inhabited by Fakeers and Byragis of various classes, who, to increase their accommodation, have built up mud walls between the pillars of the verandahs, rendering the interior extremely dark, while the accumulated smoke of a thousand years' cooking has blackened the whole so as to increase the gloom, and has also encrusted over the sculpture in such a manner as to render its details almost invisible.

There is also considerable difficulty in gaining admission to the inhabited caves, and I found it impossible to effect an entrance into the finest of the whole series, which by the way does not seem to have been discovered by either of the gentlemen above-mentioned, and which I stumbled on by chance while wandering about without any guide. It is now inhabited by the chief of the Fakeers, whom I saw preparing to cook his dinner, and who was extremely insolent when I attempted to parley with him on the subject, so that I was obliged to content myself with an imperfect survey from above.

The caves on the Udyagiri (hill of the rising sun) are entirely Buddhist, and of a very early and pure type; those on the other hill, the Khandagiri, are much later, and principally Jaina.

The earliest of the whole series is the so-called Hathi Gumpha, or elephant cave. It is a large natural cavern, the only one in those ills, and very slightly, if at all improved by art, and consequently was probably the earliest chosen as a residence by some Bauddha ascetic; and it is not improbable that it is to the sanctity acquired by some early saint, who took up his abode in it, that we owe the subsequent excavations in the hill. It is on the face of the rock above this cave that there exists the long inscription in the Lath character, which first attracted the attention of Mr. Stirling and his enthusiastic companion Major Mackenzie, and which Mr. Prinsep subsequently deciphered, (as far as its imperfect state would allow,) and published in the sixth volume of his Journal. Unfortunately, the inscription contains no name that has been identified in any of the lists, and as there is no date, we are left entirely to the character of the letters, and its internal evidence, for an approximative era in which it could have been written.

There does not appear much reason to doubt the correctness of the etymological grounds on which Mr. Prinsep assumed the date to be somewhat subsequent to the Asoka inscriptions in the same neighbourhood. At least, I do not know of one reason that can be urged for assigning it a higher antiquity. But as it would take up too much space here to enter into all the arguments that might be urged on this head, I shall content myself with stating, that I think the balance of evidence inclines to a date about two hundred years before Christ, and that cannot be very far from the truth.

The other caves on this hill have all inscriptions in the Lath character, and therefore may all be safely assigned to a date anterior to the Christian era, and probably between that and the date above given. The only apparent exception is that on the Ganes Gumpha, which is in the Kutila character of the tenth century of our era; but the cave in which it is engraved is so entirely of the same character as the rest, both in architecture and sculpture, that it cannot be assigned to a different era, and the inscription must be considered as marking its conversion to the Brahmanical faith. All the larger ones consist of a pillared verandah, of from six to ten feet in width, the length varying with the number of cells which open into it from behind, these being generally about six feet wide. In the Thakoor cave, (the large one above alluded to, to which I could not obtain admittance,) the colonnade is the longest here, being fifty-five feet in length, with wings extending at right angles to it in front.

In the Ganes Gumpha, which is perhaps the most beautiful of the series, the verandah is thirty feet long by six feet wide, and seven in height; there are four doors which open from it into the inner excavation, which is seven feet six inches deep, and of the same length as the verandah. In this instance it is not divided into separate cells[1].

The sculpture on this cave is superior to anything I have seen in India, and I wish much it could be cleaned and casts taken of it. It consists of a frieze at the back of the verandah, broken into two compartments by the heads of the doors. A representation of it is published in the seventh volume of the Journal of the Asiatic Society, p. 683, but Mr. Kittoe's sketch was a very hurried one, and the lithography is not the most perfect, so that it does not do the subject justice.

The only sculpture I am aware of that resembles it in India, is that

[1] Plate No. 1.

of the Sanchi Tope, near Bhilsa, and it resembles European art more than any other. There are no gods, no figures of different sizes, nor any extravagance; everything is in keeping and in good taste.

Some have only two intercolumniations in front, and by far the greater number only one, or to speak more correctly, consist of an outer cave communicating with the inner by a small door, and in one instance, the rock containing a small cave has been sculptured into the form of a tiger's head, whose gaping mouth forms the vestibule to the cell; I do not know of any other instance of a similar vagary.

On the Khandagiri the caves are much less interesting, being all of an evidently later date. One called Lelat Indra Kesari ka Noor, probably was excavated by that prince, and its date therefore will be the beginning of the seventh century; it is an excavation of no great extent, and it is not easy to make out from the very unfinished state in which it has been left, for what purpose it was designed, being extremely unlike all the others of the series.

As Lelat Indra, however, was a devout worshipper of Siva, and built, or at least finished the great temple at Bobaneswar, it was probably intended to be a Brahmanical cave, like those at Ellora or Elephanta; his Rani, however, was a follower of Buddha, and this may have been her work.

Close to it is the largest cave on this hill; like most others, it consists of a verandah with pillars and a long apartment parallel to it, to which has recently been added an outer verandah of masonry plastered and painted. In this cave are sculptured the images of the twenty-four Thirthankars, and their female energies, which are probably coeval with its excavation, and at one end an image of the monkey-god Hanuman, though he probably is of a later date; he was however too well covered with red paint for me to make out from the style of sculpture to what age he belonged.

None of the other caves on this hill are particularly deserving of notice. On the top of it stands a small Jain temple erected during the the supremacy of the Maharatta; a neat building, but, as might be expected from the character of its founders, of no great pretensions.

One of the most singular features in all the Buddhist caves here, is the total absence of all images of Buddha, and indeed of any apparent object of worship; a circumstance which alone would, I conceive, be sufficient to place them in a higher antiquity than any series in Western India; for it is tolerably certain that the adoration of images, and particularly of that of the founder of the religion, was the introduction of a later and more corrupt era, and unknown to the immediate followers of the deified.

Whatever sculpture is used in these caves, and they contain some of a very high class, is purely ornamental, and has no reference either to the worship of Buddha, or to the purposes for which these caves were excavated[1].

Another singularity is the absence of a Chaitya cave, though it is mentioned in the inscription on the Hathi Gumpha, "the King Aira (?) caused to be constructed subterranean chambers, caves containing a Chaitya temple and pillars." In this instance, however, the cave, if one ever existed, may have been destroyed by those who have quarried stone here for the building of the Bobaneswar and other temples in the neighbourhood. But I am more inclined to think that the Chaitya here was a structural building, probably standing on the summit of Khandagiri hill, and that it has consequently been destroyed, like most of its congeners in India, in the struggles between the Buddhists and Brahmans, its materials removed, and probably a portion of them employed in constructing the present fane.

It is more than probable that it was in the Daghopa attached to these caves, that the famous tooth relic was preserved; which, during the troubles consequent on the invasion of the Yavanas, was removed for safety to Ceylon in the beginning of the fourth century, where it, or its representative, still exists.

I may also remark, that though all the roofs of the caves are flat, and flat architraves run in every instance from one pillar to another in the verandahs, still the early Buddhists could not get over their singular predilection for the arch, and have employed it as an ornament whenever it could be introduced; and thus, though all the doors are square-headed, scarcely any exist that have not a semicircular or rather horseshoe ornament above, placed in the manner of a discharging arch in common masonry. I call this singular, for though the form of the arch is almost universal in all Buddhist caves, it does not, that I am aware of, exist in any Brahmanical one, nor in any structural building in Hindustan prior to the Mahomedan invasion, nor then in almost any Hindu building down to the present time, with the exception of some temples built during the reign of Akbar the Great.

There are not, as far as I am aware of, any other caves on the eastern side of India, certainly none of any importance, except those at Mahavellipore, which being the most modern in India, I will describe last, having previously made the circuit of the peninsula; and we must therefore step at once to the western side, where they exist of a size and magnificence totally unknown on the eastern side. I have

[1] In one cave, the Jodey Gumpha, some figures seem to be worshipping the Bo Tree; see Kittoe's plate above referred to.

not been able to visit all the caves myself, but I have examined those of Ajunta, Karli, Salsette, Doomnar, Ellora, Elephanta, and Mahavellipore. The caves of Nasik, Junir, and Baug, I have not been able to visit, but from all I could learn on the spot, the two first mentioned series contain no type not seen at Karli, Ellora, or Salsette; while the latter are so similar to those at Ajunta, that though extremely numerous, and no doubt interesting, I am not aware of their offering any thing of a new or distinctive character.

In attempting to describe so many caves, it would be desirable, if possible, to adopt some mode of classification by which to connect so many dissimilar objects. The most desirable would certainly be a chronological one, describing each cave according to its date; but their ages are so imperfectly ascertained, that this would at present, I fear, only lead to confusion; and as each series extends through several hundred years, some nearly a thousand, and consequently, they were contemporary one with another, no succession can be made out between the different series. I shall therefore describe those I have visited in the order in which I have named them above, placing Ajunta first, because it is the most perfect and complete series of Buddhist caves in India, without any admixture of Brahmanism, and contains types of all the rest; next Karli, which, though by no means so extensive as the first, is still purely Buddhistical, and contains the finest Chaitya cave in India. The Salsette or Kannari caves are also purely Bauddha, but very inferior in every respect to the two former. Those of Doomnar and Ellora contain a strong admixture of Brahmanism, and those of Elephanta are entirely Brahmanical, though perhaps not later than some of those at Ellora.

And lastly, I will revert to those at Mahavellipore, which are entirely Brahmanical, and excavated after all the other series were finished.

After crossing the valley of the Taptee from the north, you approach a ghát of some five or six hundred feet in height, supporting the table-land of the Dekkan. The upper line of the ghát is flat and regular and the wall, if I may use the expression, tolerably even except in some places where it is broken by ravines, which extend for a considerable way into the table-land above. It is in one of these ravines that the caves of Ajunta are situated. The entrance to the ravine is nearly half a mile in width, but is gradually narrower as you wind up it, till it terminates in a cascade of seven falls, called the sat koond; the

[1] See Transactions of Bombay Literary Society, vol. ii., p. 194.

lowest fall may be one hundred feet high, the others together one hundred more.

Immediately below the fall the ravine makes a sudden turn to the right, and it is in the perpendicular cliff forming the outer side of the bend, and facing the koond, that the caves are situated; the whole series extending, as nearly as I can guess, about five hundred yards from north to south-east.

The most ancient are situated about one-third of this distance, or about one hundred and fifty yards from the most northern end, and are the lowest down in the rock, not being above thirty or forty feet above the bed of the torrent, while to the north they rise to about eighty feet, and at the southern extremity they rise to about one hundred or one hundred and fifty feet; the extreme excavations however are at this end unapproachable, in consequence of the ledge of the stratum, which formed the terrace of communication along the whole series, having fallen away, and left the face of the cliff perpendicular for its whole height, which is as nearly as I could estimate about three hundred feet.

Names have been given to some of the caves, but these are neither very appropriate nor well understood, and as the local cicerone who accompanied me the first day gave the same name to different caves at different times, and, I believe, invented others when his memory failed him, I adopted the surer plan of using numbers; and, beginning at the northern end, or that lowest down the stream, called the first cave number one, and so on to twenty-seven, which is the last accessible cave at the south-eastern extremity; and as this plan can lead to no confusion, I shall now follow it.

According to this arrangement, the ninth, tenth, nineteenth, and twenty-sixth, from the north end, are Chaitya or Daghopa vaulted caves, without cells; the rest are all Viharas, or Monasteries, with cells and flat roofs.

The lowest down and the most ancient, are the twelfth and eleventh; the first-named is the plainest cave of the series, being entirely without pillars, and there is no sanctuary or image, nor, apparently, any visible object of worship; indeed, its only ornament consists of seven horseshoe canopies on each side, four of which are over the doors of the cells, the other three merely ornamental; they are very similar to those at Cuttack, and under them is a reeded string course, similar to that used in those caves, and which I have not observed any where else except there and at the great Karli cave; indeed, it resembles the caves in the Udyagiri in almost every respect, except it being square, thirty-six feet seven inches each way, while those at Cuttack are all longer than their depth. The front would have afforded the best means of identification, but unfortunately it is entirely removed by the rock above giving way; I searched earnestly for inscriptions, but could only find one on the inner wall, in a character slightly modified from that on the laths, and, therefore, probably written early in the Christian era; but it does not, from its position, seem to be at all integral, or to form a part of the original design, and therefore would not fix the date even if deciphered.

The next cave to the north, number eleven, is not quite so large, being only thirty-seven feet ten inches, by twenty-eight feet six inches; it is very similar in some respects to the last, but has four pillars in the centre supporting the roof[1].

This is, probably, one of the earliest instances of the introduction of pillars for such a purpose, and though they are clumsily used here, the example is interesting, as it was to the extended use of them, that we owe all the magnificence of the modern Vihara; the window on each side of the door is divided into three lights, by two pillars standing on each cill[2]. The sanctuary is not finished, and, indeed, seems to have been an afterthought; but there are antelopes, lions, and a boy in an attitude of prayer, sculptured on the wall in the very best style of art, and evidently coeval with those of the Ganesa Gumpha at Cuttack; the walls have been stuccoed and painted, but the paintings are so much destroyed as to be scarcely distinguishable; I could discover no inscription on any part of it.

The next two caves to these on the north side, numbers ten and nine, are two Daghopa caves, almost counterparts of one another, except that the first is very much the largest, being ninety-four feet six inches in depth, and forty-one feet three inches wide, while the other measures only forty-five feet by twenty-three feet.

The largest one has, or rather had, twenty-nine pillars surrounding the nave; they are plain octagons, without capital or base, and have been covered with stucco and painted; thirteen of them are fallen, leaving large gaps in some places, and the outer screen is entirely gone. Like all Daghopa caves, it has a ribbed roof. In some caves, the ribbing is in stone, in others, as at Karli, it is in wood. This cave combines both methods, the aisles being of stone, while the nave has been ornamented with wood, which has entirely disappeared, except some of the battens and pins that fastened it to the rock, and the footings for the ribs, which are sunk to some depth in the rock.

The Daghopa is plain and solid, without any ornament, except the square capital or toe on the top, but there can be no doubt that it was

[1] Plate No. 5, fig. 1.

[2] Fig. 2.

once richly ornamented, probably in wood, for which some mortices remain; and that it was crowned, as at Karli, by three umbrellas.

The whole of this cave has been covered with stucco and painted, and many of the smaller paintings on the pillars, and in the panels of the roof of the aisles, remain, consisting of figures of Buddha and his disciples in various attitudes, rosettes and other ornaments; but owing to the ruined state of the front, the rain apparently has beat in, and destroyed the larger subjects. There are several inscriptions painted on the plaster, and though none remain sufficiently entire to be transcribed, yet sufficient remains to show, that the characters are those that were used subsequent to the Christian era.

On the exterior face, however, of the cave, but very high up, is an inscription of some length in the pure Lath character, which would at once give an antiquity to the excavation of about 100 or 200 B. C., as far as such evidence can be relied on.

The smaller cave had only twenty pillars surrounding the nave, similar to those in the other; eight of them are broken, but at the entrance there are four pillars of a different form and richer detail. Of its paintings but little remains, except in the inner wall, where they are still tolerably entire. In this circle I found two inscriptions painted on the stucco on the walls; the first under a figure seated on a chair, with the fore finger of the left hand touching that of his right, the second under a Daghopa, painted also on the wall. And on the south side of the cave, opposite the first, there was a third inscribed in a panel under another figure, seated in a chair, but so defaced, that I could only see that it was in the same character as the other two; its existence, however, appeared to me very valuable, from its position as an integral portion of the design which it forms a part of, and if its age can be determined, it will show the period at which the paintings were executed. I have not myself much difficulty in assigning it, on the faith of Mr. Prinsep's alphabets, to the second or third century of our era.

The eighth cave from the end is merely a natural cavern, without any inscription or object of interest; and the seven that precede it, are so modern, that I would prefer going back to number thirteen, and continue to describe them as they occur from this point towards the southern extremity, as I shall thus preserve something like the succession of dates in which they were excavated, without the confusion that would arise from selecting here and there.

Thirteen is only a small cave with two cells, and has nothing remarkable about it.

Fourteen is a large unfinished cave under thirteen, and apparently meant as an under story to it; only the first line of the pillars in the interior is hewn out, and left in a rough state. The verandah pillars, however, are finished, and are of an unusual form, from being merely square piers with plain bands.

Fifteen is a plain square cave, but filled up with mud and debris nearly to the roof, so that there is considerable difficulty in effecting an entrance, and only its general plan can be made out.

Numbers sixteen and seventeen are the two finest Viharas of the series, and apparently belong to, and were excavated at the same time, with nineteen, which is the best finished Chaitya cave of the series; to these may be added the one beyond number twenty, as they all seem of the same age, and the four together form the most interesting group of the Ajunta caves. There are two long inscriptions on the external faces of sixteen and seventeen, which probably contain something of their dates and history[1]; I did not, however, attempt to copy either, and my opinion of their age, therefore, rests entirely on their architectural details and their position in the series; I believe them to have been excavated between the fourth and sixth century after Christ, but more probably about the latter date.

Sixteen is a square cave, sixty-seven feet six inches wide, and sixty-five feet two inches deep, exclusive of the sanctuary; the centre hall is surrounded by twenty pillars, generally of an octagon form, the sides of which are adorned in painting with something like a Roman scroll, alternating with wreaths of flowers[2].

All the details of its architecture are particularly good and elegant, more so than any other cave in this series; there are no side chapels, but eighteen cells surrounding the great hall. The figure in the sanctuary is seated with his feet down; some of the paintings are tolerably entire and extremely interesting, though not so much so as those in the next cave; the swords in the soldiers' hands are shaped something like the Nepalese Kookry, and the shields are of an oblong form.

Seventeen, generally called the Zodiac cave, very much resembles the last described in almost every respect. Its dimensions are sixty-four feet by sixty-three feet, and it has twenty pillars disposed as in the other; it is not, however, so lofty, and the details of the pillars are by no means so graceful or elegant as in number sixteen. The paintings, however, are much more entire, and though the colours in some places are a good deal faded, the subjects can generally be made out.

On the right hand wall, as you enter, a procession is painted.

[1] Journal of the Asiatic Society of Bengal, Vol. v. Plate 29.

[2] Plate No. 6.

Three elephants issuing from a portal, one black, one red or rather brown, and the third a white one, which seems the principal one of the group; showing how early arose the predilection for these animals, which still exists among the Burmese and Siamese of the present day. Chattahs and flags are borne before them, and men with spears, swords, and shields make up their retinue.

On the back wall is a hunting scene, in which a maned lion, powerfully and well-drawn, forms the principal object of attraction; there are also deer and dogs, and men on horseback and on foot without number.

In the verandah to this cave are some singularly interesting paintings; at one end a circular one, which I at first took for a zodiac, though, on further examination, I gave up the idea; its centre is divided in eight compartments, and the outer circle into sixteen or seventeen. Each of these compartments are crowded with small figures, but what the subject is I could not make out.

Over the door are eight figures sitting cross-legged; the first four are black, the fifth fairer, the next still more so, the last fair and wearing a crown. It may be remarked, that there are more black people painted in this cave than in any of the others: the women, however, are generally fair, and the men all shades, from black to a European complexion. The roof is painted in various patterns, not at all unlike those still existing in the baths of Titus, though in an inferior style of art. I had not time, even if I had had the ability, to copy these interesting paintings, and I fear any one who now visits them will find that much that I saw has since disappeared.

The style of these paintings cannot of course bear comparison with European painting of the present day; but they are certainly superior to the style of Europe during the age in which they were executed: the perspective, grouping, and details are better, and the story better told than in any paintings I know of, anterior to Orgagna and Fiesole. The style, however, is not European, but more resembles Chinese art, particularly in the flatness and want of shadow; I never, however, even in China, saw anything approaching its perfection.

I looked very attentively at these paintings, to try and discover if they were fresco paintings, or merely water colours laid on a dry surface; but was unable to decide the point: the colour certainly is in some cases absorbed into the plaster, and I am inclined to think they may have been painted when it was first laid on, and consequently moist; but I do not think it could have been done on the modern plan of painting each day all the plaster laid on that day.

Eighteenth. Merely a porch of two pillars, apparently the commencement of an excavation, or of a passage or entrance to

The Chaitya cave, number nineteen[1], which is more remarkable for the beauty and completeness of its details than for its size, being only forty-six feet four inches, by twenty-three feet seven inches in width. Seventeen pillars surround the nave, all of which are very richly ornamented, and above them is a band occupying exactly the same position as a triforium would in a Christian church, and occupied here with niches containing alternately figures of Buddha sitting cross-legged, and standing. The roof is ribbed in stone, but the most interesting feature is the Daghopa, which has here the three umbrellas in stone rising till they touch the roof; in front of the Daghopa is a figure of Buddha, standing. The exterior of this cave is as rich as the interior, and though damaged in some parts, by the rocks falling from above, the injury is less than in most others, and very little labour would free the lower part from the accumulated materials, and display entire one of the most perfect specimens of Buddhist art in India; but one that I must not dwell on longer, as I feel that, without drawings, I should be unable to convey to others any correct impression of its beauties or details.

Twenty. The last of this group is a small Vihara of singular plan, twenty-eight feet two inches wide, by twenty-five feet six inches deep, with two cells on each side. There is no internal colonnade, but the roof is supported by advancing the sanctuary about seven feet into the hall, and making its front consist of two columns in antis. There is also a verandah in front, with an apartment at each end. Its paintings are almost entirely obliterated, except those on the roof, and these consist of frets and flowers, not otherwise interesting than merely as showing its connexion with the Viharas sixteen and seventeen. There is an inscription on one of the pillars of the verandah, but very much obliterated, and apparently not integral.

Before proceeding further in this direction we must return back to the seventh and sixth from the north, and which, though scarcely coeval with the last group described, are certainly later than those first mentioned, and as certainly earlier than the group which succeeds, and which closes our list; but whether they are antecedent to numbers sixteen and twenty, or slightly posterior to them, I am unable to decide.

Number seven is merely a large verandah, sixty-three feet four inches in length, by thirteen feet seven inches in breadth, with the cells opening at the back of it, something in the manner of the Cuttack caves; the front line of the verandah is broken by the projection of two porches of two pillars each, which are here particularly inte-

[1] Plate No. 3.

resting, as they are extremely similar to the pillars at Elephanta, and those in the Doomar Lena at Ellora, and therefore probably not far distant in date. There is also a chapel with two pillars at each end.

To the left of the sanctuary are five crosslegged figures, each seated on a lotus, and a lotus between each; on the right, two cross-legged and seven standing figures, the centre lotus of each series supported by figures with snake canopies. Within the sanctuary, on each side, are two large and one smaller figures, and two men sitting cross-legged, and having chowries in their hands. On the step are sixteen figures of disciples seated cross-legged.

Number six is the only two-storied cave at Ajunta. The upper story has twelve pillars, octagons changing into plain squares at top and bottom, and with bold bracket capitals, not painted but sculptured with figures of Buddha. At first I thought this a Jaina cave, and tried to find the twenty-four thirthankars in some place, but was unsuccessful; the series consist of sixteen, eight, four, and are apparently of disciples, as none had the emblems by which the thirthankars are usually recognised.

The cave is fifty-three feet square, the aisles nine feet wide. The lower story is of the same dimensions as the upper, and of the same plan, except that four additional pillars have been introduced in the centre; they are all plain octagons, changing to sixteen sides, with pilasters to each row. Seven of these only are standing, nine having fallen down, owing to the inferiority of the rock in which they are cut, and also to water entering from above, and rotting the stone; the whole cave has a dismal and ruinous look not common here; and it is also without sculpture, having apparently depended entirely on painting for its decoration. The pillars in front of the sanctuary are of the same Elephanta character as those of the last-mentioned cave.

There now only remains to be described the last group of these caves, consisting of the first five from the north, and the last seven at the other extremity; they are all so nearly of the same age, that I am quite unable to discriminate between them, and all evidently the last excavated here. They are singularly unlike any other caves or structural buildings I am acquainted with, and I had consequently less means here than with the others of coming to a satisfactory conclusion regarding their dates; if, however, we assume the last group to have extended to the sixth or seventh century of our era, these must range between that period and the tenth, after which time I conceive no Buddhist caves were excavated in India, and we cannot therefore be far wrong in placing them in the eighth and ninth centuries.

As I cannot fix their succession, I may as well begin with number one, and passing over those already described, proceed to twenty-seven, the last visited.

The first that commences, or rather ends, the series on the north, is a very handsome vihara cave, with a fine verandah ninety-eight feet in length, and a chapel at each end, the hall is sixty-four feet square, adorned with twenty pillars three feet in diameter, richly carved, and with bracket capitals. The cave is a good deal filled up with mud, but, notwithstanding, the paintings are tolerably entire, and some of them very interesting; though both they and the details of the architecture are small and frittered away, when compared with the two first-described groups.

The second is a twelve-pillared cave of which I have given a plan[1]; it is in very good preservation, and the paintings, particularly on the pillars, are tolerably perfect. In the sanctuary there is a statue, of course of Buddha, and a chapel on each side of it, at the end of the aisles. In the one on the north are two most portly, fat figures, a male and female: in the south one, two male figures, occupying a like position. Who they were meant to represent I could not make out, for they were quite strangers to me.

The third is a very fine bold cave, and one of the largest viharas of the series, but does not appear to have been quite finished; the colonnade in the centre consists of twenty-eight pillars, (the only instance I know of such magnificence,) disposed in four ranges of eight pillars each, counting the angular ones in each line; the pillars, generally bold octagons eleven feet in circumference; the whole hall is ninety-one feet square; the aisles twelve feet two inches wide, which is also the width of the verandah. This cave never having been finished does not appear ever to have been painted. It is now so dreadfully infested with bats that it is almost impossible to stay in it any length of time, and I had not the courage to explore its cells; as, however, I found nothing of interest in any of the others, I do not suppose there was much to regret here.

The fourth cave is situated higher up in the face of the rock, and as there is no path to it, I did not discover its existence till the day I was leaving the place, when I saw it from the opposite side of the ravine which I had scrambled up to in a wild-goose chase, to look for the city of Lenapore, having been delighted with its name, and convinced, in spite of the assurance of my guides, that it must contain something of interest; it was, however, "vox et præterea nihil."

The fifth was so choked up with mud, that it was almost impossible

[1] Plates No. 2 and 7.

to see what it was, further than that it had been a square cave of no great dimensions.

We must now return to cave number twenty, the last described towards the south.

Leaving it you proceed for some distance along the ledge, which, owing to a torrent coming over here during the rains, is more than usually ruined, and the path in some places very narrow and dangerous; and as I had to traverse this several times in the middle of the day at the end of March. I suffered extremely, not only from the heat of the sun, but from the reflection from the rocks, which were heated like an oven.

Having passed this, however, you arrive at the twenty-first cave from the north end, a large vihara, fifty-two feet six inches deep, by fifty-one feet six inches in width. It is similar in almost every respect of plan, style, and execution, to the cave above described as number two. It is, not, however, quite finished, as the pillars of the sanctuary are only hewn rough out of the rock, and many of the details are left incomplete. Its paintings are now nearly obliterated, except on the wall on your left hand as you enter, where there still exists a large figure of Buddha, of a black complexion, or at least very dark, and with red hair, and attended by black slaves. There are several ladies introduced into the composition, but notwithstanding the blackness of their companions, they are here, as in most other caves, represented with complexions almost as fair as Europeans. There is a small chapel with two pillars in antis, on each side, as well as at each end of the lateral aisles. The verandah has fallen down, but the chapels at each end remain, with the pilaster which terminated the colonnade at each end, showing its dimensions and depth.

As I before remarked, the execution of this cave, as well as of number two, is decidedly inferior to that of the intermediate ones; not indeed in richness and quantity of ornament, but in style. There is a weakness in the drawing of the details, and the ornaments are crowded and cut up in a manner that gives a tawdry and unsatisfactory appearance to the whole; very unlike the bold magnificence of those of an earlier age. To use a comparison drawn from the architecture of our own country, they bear the same relation to numbers sixteen, seventeen, and twenty, as the Tudor architecture does to the pure Gothic of the Third Edward.[1]

The twenty-second is a small cave only seventeen feet square, without pillars, excepting two rough-hewn ones in front of the sanctuary, in which is a figure of Buddha seated, with his legs down.

[1] Compare Plates No. 6 and 7.

The twenty-third is another vihara of twelve pillars, very similar in all respects to numbers two and twenty-one; it has, however, been left in a very unfinished state, without even an image in the sanctuary, or indeed anywhere else, and there exists no trace of painting that I could detect in any part. Its dimensions are fifty-one feet by fifty-one feet eight inches.

Number twenty-four is the pendant in the series to number three, and would have been one of the finest had it been finished; but merely its general form and dimensions have been made out. Only one pillar has been completely sculptured, and one side of the colonnade exists as a wall with slits in it. It was intended to have been a twenty-pillar cave; the centre hall would have been about forty-three feet square, and the whole about seventy-four feet each way. The details of sculpture and style are of the same class as two, three, and twenty-one, but much more pains appears to have been taken with their execution, and on the whole they are richer than those above alluded to, if it is fair to judge by what is visible; for besides that so little has been executed, the cave is now half filled with mud. The verandah has been completed, but three out of its six columns are broken, and the others much injured.

This cave is particularly interesting as showing the whole process of excavation, from its commencement to the finishing of the details, some parts having been left in every stage of advancement. The rock (amygdaloidal trap) in which they are cut is of a soft, coarse texture, so that the labour of excavation could not have been so great as is generally supposed; indeed, I am very much inclined to believe that this mode of excavating was the cheapest and least laborious by which buildings of this class could be erected. If the stones were quarried so as to be of use for building purposes at the same time, it certainly would be so; but that does not seem to have been the case here, as all the rough work appears to have been done with the pick-axe.

Twenty-five. A small rude vihara cave, with a verandah of ten pillars.

Twenty six is the fourth vaulted or chaitya cave of this series, and decidedly the most modern. In general plan it is very similar to number nineteen, but its dimensions exceed the former very considerably, the whole width being thirty-six feet three inches, that of the nave seventeen feet seven inches, and the total length sixty-six feet one inch. Its sculptures, too, are far more numerous and more elaborate, indeed, more so than in any other cave of the series; but they are very inferior both in design and in execution, so much so that if other proof were wanting this alone would be sufficient to stamp this at once as one of the latest, if not the last executed cave of Ajunta.

The Buddha on the front of the Daghopa is seated with his feet down.

The walls of the aisles are entirely covered with sculpture, principally figures of Buddhas or disciples, of all sizes, and in every Buddhist position. Among others in the south aisle is one twenty-three feet long, reclining at all his length, being the attitude in which they prepare to receive nirvana (beatitude); above him are an immense host of angels, awaiting apparently his arrival in heaven, and one beating most vigorously a big drum.

The fat figures with judges' wigs, who do duty as brackets, have here four arms, which is the only instance I am aware of in these or any other Buddhist caves, of such a piece of Hinduism.

The details of the pillars, particularly those of the verandahs, are of precisely the same character as all those of this group, but their details are worse executed here, than in any of the others.

There are two inscriptions on the outside of the cave apparently integral, one under a figure of Buddha on your left as you enter, the other is much broken but more distinct, upon your right. The character used in them belongs to the ninth or tenth century of the Christian era.

The twenty-seventh cave is a small square vihara without pillars, and the sanctuary only commenced, and the whole left in a very unfinished state; the front has entirely crumbled away, so that its dimensions can scarcely be ascertained; it was, however, about forty feet in width.

There are one or two caves beyond this, but the ledge having fallen away, they are quite inaccessible. From the ruined state of their fronts, and the debris that has accumulated before them, I was unable to guess either at their size or state of progress; judging, however, from the last caves visited, there cannot be much worth seeing in them, and indeed, I am not quite sure that what I took for caves were not holes, or shadows thrown by masses of rock.

I have been more particular in describing this series than any other, partly because I am not aware that any detailed account of them has been given to the public to which I could refer, and partly because they are in some respects the most interesting series of Buddhist caves in India. They cannot, indeed, boast of a chaitya cave like Karli, but the viharas here are more splendid than anywhere else; they are more entire, and are the only caves that retain much of their original painting and decoration. They also are purely a Buddhist series, and almost every change in cave architecture can be traced in them during a period of about one thousand or twelve hundred years, which is nearly the term during which that religion flourished in its native land; and they thus form a sort of chronometric scale, which I found extremely useful in my attempts to ascertain the ages and dates of caves in other series, none of which are so complete as this one.

The others having all been described before, I shall merely notice such peculiarities as bear specially upon my subject, and refer to printed descriptions for details.

BAUG.

In a small valley or ravine penetrating, like that at Ajunta, into a table-land resting on the ghât on the north side of the valley of the Taptee, and about three miles from the small town of Baug, are situated four caves, which have been described by Lieutenant Dangerfield in the second volume of the Transactions of the Literary Society of Bombay. His description is remarkably clear, and with the drawings that accompany it, enable one to determine at once what they are, and almost the age at which they were excavated.

The largest vihara would at Ajunta be a "twenty-pillar" cave, but owing to the badness of the rock in which it is excavated, the architect left four additional columns in the centre of the hall. In the sanctuary there is a daghopa, an arrangement I do not know of elsewhere, and can only account for here, by supposing that this symbol was necessary for Buddhist worship, and there being no chaitya cave in the series it was necessary to introduce it here; in that case, however, it is strange that they omitted the figure of Buddha in front, which seems to have been the case.

The second cave is an unfinished one, but the third, at some distance from the two first, is a vihara eighty feet by sixty, and though much ruined retains a good deal of its original paintings; judging from them, the only detail given, they appear to be of about the same age as the second group at Ajunta, whilst the large cave belongs to the last of that series, or may be intermediate between the two.

There are two other caves at Baug, but one entirely ruined, the other only commenced.

KARLI.

About half way between Poona and Bombay on the right hand side of the valley as you proceed towards the sea, is situated the great cave of Karli, without exception the largest and finest Chaitya cave in India, and fortunately also the best preserved.

Its interior dimensions are one hundred and two feet three inches or total length, eighty-one feet three inches for length of nave. Its breadth from wall to wall is forty-five feet seven inches, while the width of the nave is twenty-five feet seven inches[1]. The nave is separated from the side aisles by fifteen columns on each side, of good design and workmanship; on the abacus which crowns the capital of each of these are two kneeling elephants, and on each elephant are two seated figures, generally a male and female, with their arms over each other's shoulders; but sometimes two female figures in the same attitude. The sculpture of these is very good, and the effect particularly rich and pleasing. Behind the Chaitya are seven plain octagonal piers without sculpture, making thus thirty-seven pillars altogether; the Chaitya is plain, and very similar to that in the large cave at Ajunta, but here, fortunately, a part of the wooden umbrella which surmounted it remains. The wooden ribs of the roof, too, remain nearly entire; and the framed screen, filling up a portion of the great arch in front, like the centering of the arch of a bridge, (which

[1] In the Atlas to Lord Valentia's Travels, a detailed plan of this cave is given, on which the dimensions taken by the scale are forty-six feet wide by one hundred and twenty-six feet long; and as the plan appears to have been drawn with considerable care, (by Mr. Salt, I believe,) and these figures are repeated in the text, I was a good deal staggered by finding so great a discrepancy, and inclined at first to give up my own as incorrect. I have however retained them, not only because they were taken with care, and I cannot see how so great an error could have crept into them; but also, because Lord Valentia's dimensions are quite at variance with those of all the Chaitya caves I am acquainted with, as the following table will show.

	Length.	Width.				
No. 10, at Ajunta, is	94·6	41·3	or as	1	to	2·285
Cave at Karli, is	102·3	45·7	„	1	„	2·243
Kannari, is	88·6	39·10	„	1	„	2·222
No. 19, Ajunta, is	46·4	23·7	„	1	„	1·961
No. 9, Ajunta, is	45·	23·	„	1	„	1·956
Viswakarma, is	83·1	43·	„	1	„	1·939
No. 26, Ajunta, is	66·1	36·3	„	1	„	1·826

While Lord Valentia's dimensions for the Karli cave would be as 1 to 2·739.

It is not however only to confirm my own measurements that I have quoted this table, but to show on how regular a system these caves were excavated, and also as confirming their relative ages, as arrived at in the text from other grounds; for it will be observed, that the oldest caves are longest in proportion to their breadth; and that the ratio diminishes as we descend in the series in an almost perfect progression, the only apparent exception being the Kannari cave; but if that is a copy of the Karli one, as I have stated in the text, this is accounted for. If I am mistaken in placing it as a copy in the ninth century, it must on many grounds take its place as it stands in this table.

Another apparent exception is the small cave, No. 9, Ajunta, which in the text I placed in the same age as the one next it, and I confess I am at present unable to offer any suggestion to account for the discrepancy.

by the way it much resembles,) still retains the place in which it was originally placed.

At some distance in advance of the arched front of this cave is placed a second screen, which exists only here and at the great cave at Salsette; though it might have existed, and I am inclined to believe did, in front of the oldest Chaitya caves, Nos. 9 and 10, at Ajunta; it consists of two plain octagonal columns, with pilasters; over these is a deep plain mass of wall, occupying the place of an entablature, and over this again an attic, if I may use the term, of four dwarf pillars; except the lower piers, the whole of this has been covered with wooden ornaments, and by a careful examination, and measurement of the various mortices and footings, it might still be possible to make out the greater part of the design; it appears, however, as far as I could discover, to have consisted of a broad balcony in front of the plain wall, supported by bold wooden brackets from the two piers, and either roofed, or having a second balcony above it; no part of the wood however exists now, either here, or at Salsette.

It is more than probable, however, that this was the music gallery, or Nagara khana, which we still find existing in front of almost all Jaina temples, down even to the present day; whether the space between this outer and the inner screen was roofed over or not, is extremely difficult to decide; from the mortices at Salsette, I should certainly say it was so; but here the evidence is by no means so distinct, though there is certainly nothing to contradict the supposition.

I could find no traces of painting in this cave, though the inner wall has been plastered and may have been painted; but the cave is inhabited, and the continued smoke of cooking fires have so blackened its walls, that it is impossible to decide the question now; strangely enough its inhabitants are now Sivites, and the cave is considered a temple dedicated to Siva, the Daghopa performing the part of a gigantic Lingam, which it must be confessed it resembles a good deal. While I was there, there was a fair going on, and a festival in honour of his Hindu godship. All the flat spots of the rock were occupied by tents, and the dokaans of the various dealers in sweetmeats and trinkets who frequent these places; and every corner was occupied by pilgrims or devotees of some sort or other, who, though they did not actually prevent my entering or sketching, were extremely clamorous for alms, and annoyed me a good deal by their curiosity and impertinence.

It would be of great importance if the age of this cave could be positively fixed; but though that cannot quite be done, I think it probable that its age is antecedent to the Christian era; and at the same time, it cannot possibly have been excavated more than two hundred years before that era.

On the Silasthamba (pillar) on the left of the entrance, Colonel Sykes copied an inscription, which Mr. Prinsep deciphered in the sixth volume of the Journal of the Asiatic Society; it merely says, "This lion pillar is the gift of Ajimitra Ukas, the son of Saha Ravisabhoti;" the character, Prinsep thinks, that of the first or second century B.C. From its position and import, the inscription appears to be integral, and the column is certainly a part of the original design. For myself, I confess, that if the Lath character was ever in use on this side of India, I do not think it could have undergone so great a change as these characters show in so short a time, and that we must come down, at least, to the Christian era for this inscription.

In a letter lately received from Dr. Bird, of Bombay, he says, "I may mention that the one at Carlee presents an inscription of the twentieth year of Dutthama Hara, otherwise called Duttagamini, king of Ceylon, B.C. 163." I did not see this inscription; I do not know, therefore, whether it is integral or not, nor in what character it is written, which is of importance; for unless other circumstances confirm the identity, I should be afraid of being deceived by the nominal similarity of a king at so great a distance. If, however, the inscription, which Dr. B. will no doubt publish, should confirm this, it will be one of the most interesting dates that these inscriptions have yet disclosed to us.

In disposition and size, and also in detail, as far as similarity can be traced between a cave entirely covered with stucco and painted, and one which either never had, or has lost both these ornaments, this cave is so similar to the two at Ajunta which I had before placed about this age, and on the front of it there is also the reeded ornament which is so common at Khandagiri, and only exists there and in the oldest caves at Ajunta, that from all these circumstances I am inclined to think the above date 163 B.C., as at least extremely probable, though by no means as a date to be implicitly relied upon.

It is to this cave, more especially, that the remark applies that I made, p. 35, that the Chaitya caves seem at once to have sprung to perfection; for whether we adopt the Mahawanso for our guide, or Asoka's inscriptions, it is evident, that this country, under the name of Maharatthan in the former, and Pitenika in the other, is one of the unconverted countries to which missionaries were sent in the tenth year of Asoka's reign; and if, therefore, we assume the above date to be at all near the truth, a century had scarcely elapsed between the conversion of the country and the execution of this splendid monument. There is nothing in the Viharas here or elsewhere which I have placed about the same date, that might not have been elaborated from a natural cavern in that period, but there is a complication of design in this that quite forbids the supposition; and it must either be brought down to a much more modern epoch, or it must be admitted to be a copy of a structural building; and even then but half the difficulty is got over. Was that structural building a temple of the Brahmans or Buddhists? was it designed or invented since the death of Sakya Sinha? or did it belong to a former religion? and lastly, if we are correct in supposing cave digging to have commenced only subsequent to Asoka's reign, why, while the Viharas were still so small, and so insignificant, was so great a work undertaken in the rock[1]?

It would be a subject of curious inquiry to know whether the wood-work now existing in this cave is that originally put up or not. Accustomed as I had long been to the rapid destruction of every thing wooden in that country, I was half inclined to be angry when the idea first suggested itself to me, but a calmer survey of the matter has convinced me that it is; certain it is, that it is the original design, for we find it repeated in stone in all the niches of the front, and there is no appearance of change or alteration in any part of the roof; every part of it is the same as is seen so often repeated in stone in other and more modern caves, and it must therefore have been put up by the Buddhists before they were expelled; and if we allow that it has existed eight hundred or one thousand years, which it certainly has, there is not much greater improbability in its having existed near two thousand years, as I believe to be the case. As far as I could

[1] In the Mahawanso, (page 12,) it is said that the first convocation was held "in a splendid hall built at the entrance of the Sattapani cave," which would seem to prove that the cave then existed. The Mahawanso, however, was compiled one thousand years after that event, and the cave which may have been a subsequent excavation designed to mark the place where the meeting was held; or at best, it is but a tradition that such was the case.

In like manner it is mentioned in the Chinese work quoted by Colonel Sykes, in his notes on the political state of ancient India, (vol. vi., p. 203, Journal R.A.S.,) that Ananda, "after the death of Buddha, collected five hundred pious men in the cavern of Pi pho lo, and, jointly with them, collected the vinayas." This is evidently the same tradition still further improved upon, and coming from an authority so distant in date and locality, is not entitled to much respect, unless indeed some cave could be discovered of that date; or some circumstantial evidence be adduced to corroborate a tradition which may easily have sprung up from the importance which caves had assumed, as a form of Buddhist architecture, at the time these works were written.

ascertain, the wood is teak. It must be recollected, that though exposed to the atmosphere, it is protected from being wetted by the rain, it has no stress or strain upon it but from its own weight, as it does not support the roof, though it appears to do so; and the rock seems to have defied the industry of the white ants.

As this is decidedly the finest Chaitya cave in India, a few remarks on the architectural ordinance of these caves may not be misplaced.

However much they vary in size or in detail, their general arrangements, as I mentioned before, are the same in every part of India, and the mode of admitting light, which is always so important a piece of architectural effect, is in all precisely identical.

Bearing in mind that the disposition of parts is exactly the same as those of the choir of a Gothic round, or polygonal apse cathedral, the following description will be easily understood[1]. Across the front there is always a screen with a gallery over it, occupying the place of the rood-loft, on which we now place our organs: in this there are three doors; one, the largest, opening to the nave, and one to each of the side aisles; over this screen the whole front of the cave is open to the air, one vast window the whole breadth of the same section, stilted so as to be more than a semicircle in height, or generally of a horse-shoe form.

The whole light, therefore, fell on the Daghopa, which is placed exactly opposite in the place of the altar, while the colonnade around and behind, is thus less perfectly lit, the pillars there being always placed very closely together, the light was never admitted in sufficient quantities to illuminate the wall behind, so that to a person standing near the door in this direction, there appeared nothing but "illimitable gloom."

I do not conceive that a votary was ever admitted beyond the colonnade under the front, the rest being devoted to the priests and the ceremonies, as is now the case in China, and in Catholic churches, and he therefore never could see whence the light came, and stood in comparative shade himself, so as to heighten its effect considerably. Still further to increase this scenic effect, the architects of these temples have placed the screens and music galleries in front, in such a manner, as to hide the great window from any person approaching the temple; though these appear to have been omitted in later examples, as in the Viswakarma of Ellora, and the two later Chaitya caves at Ajunta, and only a porch added to the inner screen, the top of which served as the music gallery; but the great window is then exposed to view, which I cannot help thinking is a great defect. To a votary once having

[1] Plates No. 3 and No. 8.

entered the porch, the effect is the same, and if the space between the inner and outer screen was roofed, which I suppose it to have been, no one not previously acquainted with the design, could perceive how the light was admitted; supposing a votary to have been admitted by the centre door, and to have passed under the screen to the right or left, the whole arrangements were such, that an architectural effect was produced certainly superior to any thing I am acquainted with in ancient or modern temples.

Something of the same sort is attempted in the classic and modern Hindu temples, where the only light is admitted by the door directly facing the image, which is thus lit up with considerable splendour, and the rest of the temple is left in a rather subdued light, so as to give it considerable relief. The door, however, makes but a clumsy window compared with that of the Buddhist cave, for the light is too low, the spectator himself impedes a portion of it, and standing in the glare of day, unless he uses his hands to shade his eyes, he can scarcely see what is within. In the Hypœthral temples, this was probably better managed, and the light introduced more in the Buddhist manner; but we know so little of their arrangements, that it is difficult to give an opinion on a subject so little understood.

Almost all writers agree, that the Pantheon at Rome is the best lit temple that antiquity has left us; in one respect it equals our caves, that it has but one window, and that placed high up; but it is inferior, inasmuch as it is seen to every one in the temple, and that the light is not concentrated on any one object, but wanders with the sun all round the building.

I cannot help thinking that the earlier Christian architects would have reinvented this plan of lighting, had they been able to glaze so large a space; but their inability to do this forced them to use smaller windows, and to disperse them all over the building, so as to gain a sufficiency of light for their purposes; and a plan having once become sacred, it never was departed from in all the changes of style and detail which afterwards took place.

Besides the great cave, there are, of course, a number of viharas attached to it; they are, however, all of them, small, and appear very insignificant compared with its splendour. This may perhaps be, and I am inclined to think is, an evidence of their antiquity; for the Viharas seem at first to have been mere cells, "where the Arhans sat to meditate," as Fa-hian expresses it, but to have become magnificent halls and temples as we find them at Ajunta, as the religion became more corrupt.

The principal vihara here is three tiers in height, (they can scarcely be called stories;) they are plain halls with cells, but without any internal colonnades, only the upper one possesses a verandah; the lower ones may, indeed, have been constructed with this usual appendage, but great masses of the rock above have given way, and falling down, have carried with them the whole of the fronts. There are no sanctuaries, and though there are one or two relievos of Buddha sitting in the lotus, and with his legs down, they do not appear to be integral or original parts of the design.

Still further are numerous similar excavations, and some fine cisterns filled with clear spring water; near one of these is a small daghopa much ruined.

There is a small vihara on the south side of the great cave, of the same character as those on the north, but owing to the fair and crowd, my examination of these caves was much more imperfect than I could have wished. There may be some that I did not enter, and peculiarities that I did not observe in those I did. From all I saw, however, I am inclined to rank them with the earlier caves at Ajunta, and though not perhaps quite so ancient as the Udyagiri series, they cannot be much more modern; which goes far to confirm the date I have above given to the great cave.

KANNARI.

These caves being well known, having been often described before, it will not be necessary to be so detailed in my description of them, as of the Ajunta series; though they are more numerous, amounting I should think to nearly a hundred in number, they are, on the whole, much less interesting than either Ajunta, Ellora, or Karli; the great chaitya cave being very similar, though very inferior to that of the last-named series, and presenting no peculiarity not seen in the other, while none of the viharas can compare with those of the first two, either in size or design, the greater part of them consisting merely of a small square cell, with a small verandah of two columns in front.

The whole of these caves are excavated in one large bubble of a hill, situated in the midst of an immense tract of forest country. Most of the hills in the neighbourhood are covered with the jungle, but this one is nearly bare, its summit being formed by one large rounded mass of compact rock, under which a softer stratum has, in many places, been washed out by the rains, forming natural caves, which, slightly improved by art, have been appropriated as cells, some probably the first so used on the hill; it is in the stratum again below this, that most of the excavations are situated.

Approaching the caves by the usual route, the first you come to is the unfinished excavation figured and described by Salt, p. 47, Vol. I., Transactions of Literary Society of Bombay. It was intended, apparently, to have been a chaitya cave, though it has been left so incomplete that it is difficult to make out the plan; the outer porch, however, is nearly completed, and it is evident that it was not intended to have an outer music-gallery screen, like that which adorns its more ancient neighbour; and it presents but little of interest in its details, except, perhaps, that its external pillars are of the same order as those at Elephanta, and therefore probably mark it as a cotemporary example. On the whole it puts me much in mind of Lelat Indra Kesar ka noor more than any other cave I have seen, but they are both so unfinished that it is difficult to institute a comparison between them. It is, probably, the latest excavation of any importance attempted in the hill, and may date about the ninth or tenth century of Christ, probably even more modern than that.

Immediately beyond this is a group of caves, (containing among them the great chaitya cave of this series,) which I would willingly omit describing in detail, as that has been so well done by Mr. Salt, in the paper above referred to, but they contain so much that is interesting, and I may add, puzzling in their chronology, that I cannot pass them over; and to ensure greater exactitude, I shall try to combine his description with my own notes.

The first is a vihara consisting of a long irregular verandah o inferior workmanship, with cells opening at the back of it; but the point of greatest interest is, that it also contains two recesses or sanctuaries, in which stand daghopas. The three sides of the recess in which the most southern stands, are divided into panels, in which are carved one, two, or more figures of Buddha and of Bodhisatwas, in various attitudes.

Behind the northern daghopa, is a figure of Buddha seated on a Sinhasana or lion-throne placed on a lotus, the stalk of which is supported by two boys with hoods of cobra de capellos; from the stem of the lotus, two others spring, on which stand two youthful figures with chowries, and one with a lotus-bud in his hand; two flying figures above, and two priestly ones below, complete the tableau, which is found both at Karli and Ajunta, besides being frequently repeated here; but in no cave in any of these series, that could date before the third or fourth century of our era, unless, indeed, it is in such a position that it could have been added at any time. The verandah extends so closely up to the large cave, that only a partition of a few inches thick has been left between them, and which subsequently has been broken through, thus leaving an irregular hole by which you may pass from the one to the other.

The great cave[1] in almost every respect, resembles the great cave at Karli; it possesses the music-gallery screen in the same position and of the same form; and here it is still more evident, that the centre at least must have been roofed, but the roof could not have continued to the end, or it would have cut across the great figures of Buddha, twenty-three feet high, which occupy both ends; below where this roof would come, the wall is covered with sculpture, but in a very crude style of Buddhist art; indeed I do not know of a cave with anything so wretched.

The front of the cave above this roof is here quite plain and evidently not meant to have been seen; at Karli, though it must also have been nearly concealed, it is still ornamented with a series of niches; indeed, no part of that cave, seen or unseen, is slurred over as every thing is here; there is no trace of the wood-work which should have filled the great window, but over the top of the arch is a number of pins remaining; they seem, however, better fitted to hang curtains to, than to support wood-work, and I think must have been applied to the former purpose; but whether by the original diggers or not, it would not be easy to decide.

The dimensions of the interior are somewhat less than those of Karli, the total length being eighty-eight feet six inches, total breadth thirty-nine feet ten inches, the length and breadth of the nave being seventy-four feet two inches and thirty-nine feet ten inches respectively. The daghopa, forty-nine feet in circumference.

Very little of its wood-work remains, none on the daghopa, and on the roof only the tenons and battens to which the rafters were attached, and there are no remains of a screen in the great window.

The pillars that surround the nave are of the same order as those at Karli, but executed in the most slovenly manner,—the elegance of proportion is entirely lost. The figures on the capitals are much worse executed; the elephants here are in some instances employed in pouring water from jars they hold in their trunks, on daghopas, or on the bogaha, or sacred bo tree; and the boys with the snake hoods are also introduced. Only six of the columns, however, on one side, and eleven on the other, are so ornamented, and the rest were never intended to be so, as they are finished as plain octagons; which is another instance of the carelessness exhibited in this cave.

In front of the cave there is a court-yard of irregular form, (see

[1] Plate No. 3.

accompanying plan,) the front being only thirty feet wide, and not parallel to the front of the cave, while immediately beyond the Silasthambas it is thirty-six feet, and at the vestibule of the cave itself is forty-six feet including the niches.

It is extremely difficult to account for this irregularity, and the smallness of the court, which is quite inexcusable on any architectural grounds, and gives a poor appearance to the whole front. It could not have been caused by the form of the hill, as Mr. Salt supposes, and it was not till after long thought on the subject that what now appears to me to be the true solution of the problem occurred to me, namely, in the prior existence of the long vihara to the south, and of the little daghopa on its circular cave, marked E. in the plan, the whole interior surface of which is divided into panels filled with figures of the Buddha, similar to those described in the vihara on the other side of the great cave.

In describing the caves at Baug I mentioned the daghopas existing in the sanctuaries, apparently because there existed no chaitya have in the series; and believing this explanation to be the correct one, I was not a little surprised to find three daghopas existing here at the very threshold of the great Chaitya cave; and it was not till it occurred to me that they must have existed there before the great cave was begun, that I could account for the circumstance; the form of the court soon convinced me (after the idea was started), that this was the true solution: they are more ancient; and the spot having probably become particularly sacred, some devotee resolved on excavating a great temple between them; here, however, arose the difficulty. North and south, or at right angles to the axis of the hill, these caves are only thirty feet apart, and it was necessary to introduce a cave forty feet wide between them; this could only be done by commencing on the lesser dimension, and working back till he got behind them, where the cave was extended to the required width. It is quite evident that the long verandah of the southern cave never could have been allowed, had it been subsequently excavated, to approach so near the great cave as to endanger the wall breaking between them; for there is nothing to govern its length; it could have been as easily extended in one direction as the other; but the width of a chaitya cave governs all the other dimensions, and if the cave was to be of a certain class, it was necessary in the first place that it should have a certain width; and it was to obtain this it has encroached so nearly on its northern and southern neighbours. This will be more easily understood by referring to the accompanying plan.

Assuming this to be correct, we are at once met by a still greater difficulty than the one got over. When I first entered this cave, seeing its similarity in design and detail to the one at Karli, I at once concluded they were of the same age, and that the difference in execution was to be accounted for from the greater coarseness of the rock, and that it must have been designed by some provincial or inferior artist; and in every other case I know, this reasoning would have held good, for I know no instance in which an architect, Buddhist, Brahmanical, or Mahometan, has copied a building of a former age. Yet this cave seems to be the exception, and if I am not very much mistaken, it must be brought down to the ninth or tenth century of Christ.

It is also not a little singular that the execution of every detail should be so clumsy and bad; for though we find in the descending series of Buddhist structures a tendency to polytheism, and the fripperiness of ornament, I do not know any instance in which the figures and details are so bad as here, and this, too, at a time when Hindu art had scarcely passed its culminating point of perfection.

After proceeding some little distance to the northward from this group, and then turning to your right hand, you enter a narrow glen or gully, down which a strong mountain torrent pours during the rainy season. It is in the rocks that form the two sides of this glen that the greatest number of caves are situated.

The first you approach on your right hand is the so-called Durbar Cave, the finest vihara of the series, and the only one that can compete with the Ajunta ones in size; its dimensions are ninety-six feet six inches in length, forty-two feet three inches in depth, of course exclusive of the cells; the colonnade goes round only three sides, and the sanctuary occupies one intercolumniation of the inner range, as in number twenty at Ajunta. It is, however, too low for its other dimensions, being scarcely nine feet high, the pillars and plan of the same order as the Viswakarma at Ellora. The verandah has a range of eight plain octagon pillars, with pilasters. Below this is another cave, or rather series of cells, which give it the appearance of being two stories high, but there is nothing remarkable in the lower ones.

Immediately opposite there is an immense excavation, but so worn by the rain and torrent, as to look more like a natural cavern; and were it not for some fragments of columns hanging to the roof, and details in some more sheltered places, I should have supposed it to be such.

Proceeding upwards on either hand are some twenty or thirty excavations, but none worthy of particular description; some (two I think), contain daghopas, the rest are small viharas, with one or two cells and verandahs, the pillars of which are generally either entirely washed away, or very much worn, the material being soft laterite or breccia, little better than hard gravelly clay.

The first cave in this direction has some of its pillars the same as those of number seven[1] of Ajunta, and which I have seen nowhere else; it has also the cushion pillars of Elephanta. From its position, and also from the gradual progress of style in these caves, I feel inclined to think this one of the most modern, and all below it consequently more ancient, and therefore probably coeval with the group of the Ajunta eries, described as numbers sixteen and twenty.

Above these, on the south side, under the brow of the hill, is another series of viharas. They are small, but some of them, especially three, very interesting, from the walls being entirely covered with sculpture, of very fair execution; the general design of which is a Buddha seated on a lotus, the same as already described as placed behind the northern daghopa in the long cave; this is repeated here with almost no variation, and its style is so similar, that it certainly represents a form of religion and art that must be very nearly, if not quite cotemporary.

The general size of these caves is from twelve to fifteen feet square; one, however, that I paced, was about forty feet square, without pillars. It was covered with sculpture, but strange to say, there was no sanctuary, but merely one large standing figure of Buddha opposite the entrance. There were cells as usual, and benches round the sides.

It is not very easy to decide whether these caves are more modern than those below; on the whole I am inclined to think they are, though their age cannot differ much; and if so, the Kannari series will be arranged as follows: first those in the ravine, in the fourth or fifth century; those last described with those on each side of the great cave, probably at least a century later; then the great cave; and, lastly, the unfinished one first alluded to.

They may thus be considered one of the most modern of the Buddhist series in India. Indeed, I am inclined to think that the greater part of them at least were executed by a colony of Buddhists, who may have taken refuge here after being expelled from the continent, and who have tried to reproduce the lost Karli in their insular retreat.

Some remains of plaster and painting exist in almost all these caves, though from the porous nature of the stone through which the water must percolate during the rains, the vestiges are small, and I could not find one complete figure in any; owing to this cause

[1] I am not quite certain this should not be number twenty; the note was made at Salsette, and I fear the drawing was wrongly numbered: for the context it is immaterial which.

no vestige of either exists on the roofs, but only on the walls in the less exposed situations. The porosity of the rock, however, has enabled the "good monks" to furnish themselves with a copious supply of delicious water; almost every cave is furnished with a cistern or well, which even at the time of my visit in April was nearly full, though no rain could have fallen for months. Nothing of the kind exists at Ajunta, but the stream with its koonds, supplied the deficiency there; at Karli, Ellora, Elephanta, Khandagiri, and even at Gwalior, these cisterns are to be found cut in the rock, in the vicinity of all the temples and viharas.

Most of the principal Buddhas in this series sit with the feet down, only the smallest ones with their legs crossed; and very often the principal figure of a group, apparently a Bodhisatwa, is a standing one, with a high head-dress I have not remarked elsewhere, and attended by two women with chowries; the true Buddha is, I believe, always attended by men.

A good deal of masonry exists on the hill as the supporting walls of terraces, which have been formed in front of all the different series of caves, and no doubt were formerly planted with gardens, as those at Gwalior now are; and they probably existed at the other series, but have now been destroyed. The view from the upper series of terraces is very fine and interesting. On the slope above the cornice of some of these caves mortices are cut in the rock, and are evidently footings for wooden posts which may have been used to support a decoration of some sort, but more probably an awning or screen to shelter the front of the cave from the sun.

DHUMNAR.

About forty miles south-east from Neemuch, and one from the village of Chundwassa, are situated the series of caves which I will now proceed to describe.

In themselves they are small and comparatively uninteresting, and were it not for the existence of the Brahmanical rock temple behind them, would not deserve much notice; but as this was the first thing that made clear to me the distinction between Buddhist and Brahmanical rock-cut temples, and will assist in explaining the more splendid ones at Ellora, I must give such details as will enable others to understand my own impressions on the subject.

The hill of Dhumnar, like all the other hills in the neighbourhood, consists of a flat plateau of rock, surrounded by a perpendicular cliff, from the bottom of which a mass of debris forms a talus, sloping down to the plain; in the present instance the cliff is nowhere higher than twenty feet, which necessarily circumscribes the dimensions of the caves, to keep within it, thus rendering them the most diminutive series I know of in India; and besides, the rock is the most unfavourable that can be conceived for the exhibition of sculpture, the whole hill consisting of a coarse iron-stone or laterite, very similar to that of Cuttack, but here of a coarser grain than I ever before saw it.

At the bottom of the cliff a broad terrace has been formed, which still exists tolerably entire, at the end of which you enter laterally into the so-called "Child's Cave." Here the daghopa stands in the centre of a small court, in the open air; immediately behind it is the cell or sanctuary, in which is a figure of Buddha sitting cross-legged, with a male attendant on each side of him; the cell is isolated by a covered passage running round it, one side of which is occupied by a recumbent figure, about ten feet long, in the same attitude as the larger one in the most modern chaitya cave at Ajunta, described above; behind are three Buddhistical figures, sitting cross-legged, probably Bodhisatwas, or of the predecessors of the great occupant of the sanctuary. A smaller figure stands between each of these, and three more stand on the third side of the passage, probably disciples.

The next in importance is Bheem Sing ka Bazaar. It is a chaitya cave, with vaulted and ribbed roof of the usual form and detail, but here only about thirty feet deep by fifteen wide, and without side aisles. There has been a porch nearly square in front of it, but the roof has tumbled in, and now encumbers the entrance. The rock in which this cave is cut is, as in the former instance, isolated by a passage running round it; round two sides of this passage, and a small portion of the third side, there runs a square colonnaded verandah, from which open a number of small cells, thus forming a combination of a chaitya cave with a vihara, which I never saw before. The pillars were evidently intended to have been carried round the third side, but it has been left unfinished, which does not say much for its antiquity.

The next three in importance are the great and little Kutchery, and the Ranee's Abode[1]. They have all semicircular domed recesses at the inner end, with daghopas. One has a rib-vaulted roof like the bazaar, but the other two have square flat roofs divided into nine compartments, and supported by four pillars.

The other excavations are of no great extent, being merely cells from six to ten or twelve feet square, with the usual verandah in

[1] These names are taken from Colonel Tod's description of these caves in his Journal.

front; but the extreme coarseness of the rock seems to have precluded even the quantity of ornament being bestowed on them, that is usual in other series.

Counting those only commenced, and even the merest scratchings in the rock, there may be from sixty to seventy caves altogether. I could not count so many, and where therefore Colonel Tod found his hundred and seventy caves I am at a loss to conceive.

It is very difficult to form an opinion as to the age of these caves, as it has been impossible for their architects to express or define their details with any exactitude in such a pudding-stone. I have, however, no doubt that the whole were at one time plastered, and that what is now seen is merely the coring; but here again the badness of the material, by allowing the water to soak through, has peeled off every vestige of the decoration, and the figures seem to have gone through a second attack of the small-pox, which has disfigured them to an extent almost ludicrous.

As far, however, as I could judge, they must all be very modern. The similarity of style and execution in the Child's Cave to number twenty-seven of Ajunta, convinced me that they were of the same age; and in the whole of them there is want of that simplicity and majesty which distinguishes the earlier Buddhist works, and a tendency to Jainism, which exists only in the latest caves; and what architectural details I could make out by looking at them from a distance, all went to confirm this impression.

About fifty paces from the edge of the cliff, in the centre of the plateau, a pit has been dug, I thought of about fifty paces by twenty, and about forty-five feet deep. Tod, however, says a hundred feet by seventy, and thirty-five deep, (and he probably is more correct, as, contrary to my usual custom, I omitted to measure it): towards the west end of this pit a temple has been left standing; the top of the Sikra or spire being level with the plateau above. It differs in every respect from those already described, being in fact merely a model of a Brahmanical structural temple, with all the accompaniments usually found in them. Indeed, externally, the temple very much resembles those at Barolli, described by Tod, and which I had just visited. The vimana is almost a fac-simile, as far as the material would allow, though the mantapa or porch is slightly different in form, and larger in proportion. In the sanctuary is a black marble statue of Vishnu, well executed, and with all his usual attributes, and on the floor in front of him a large well-oiled Lingam, which evidently is now the principal object of worship, indicating a change of masters I have several times seen in these parts.

Around the large temple are nine smaller shrines, each of which had contained a piece of sculpture; but only three are now so occupied. One, a tablet, with six figures very much defaced; another, Vishnu reposing on the Seseja; and the third, a series of the ten avatars, but with this singularity: that here the ninth, instead of being Gotama, as in every other of the series I had then seen, is Chaturbuj himself, with his gadhi, chakra, and all his usual attributes.

In front of the temple, a long level passage, cut through the rock (a hundred and ten paces long,) leads to a valley or depression in the plateau, and was evidently formed, not only to afford a level entrance to the temple, but to allow the rain-water to drain off, which otherwise would have stagnated in the pit.

It is not very easy to understand why this passage was not brought out through the scarp, and thus access given to the temple from the plain. Perhaps it arose from an unwillingness to destroy the caves, which would have been necessary had that been attempted; and the Brahmans, unlike our northern reformers, never seem to have been destroyers. Perhaps, also, it may have arisen from the necessity of placing the temple east and west, and a consequent desire to approach it in front, and not at right angles.

The Brahmans never, it appears, were cave diggers; and when, in the struggles with the Buddhists, they thought it necessary to engage the prejudices of the people on their side, by adopting this most popular and splendid way of erecting places of worship, nothing can be more clumsy, and if I may use the expression, unnatural, than the way in which they set about it. They either copied Buddhist viharas, but without the cells that gave them meaning, and covered the walls with sculpture, which, owing to the badness of the light, they were ill-fitted to display; or, what was worse, they copied in the rock, (as in this instance,) their own structural temples; but thus necessitating their being placed in a pit, which quite destroyed their effect. Had they always been able to find isolated rocks, as they did at Mahavellipore, this remark would lose much of its force; but both the Kylas at Ellora, and this temple, are deprived of half their effect from this cause.

The Buddhist temples, on the contrary, are always in good grammar; they are all interiors,—really caves,—and with only such external ornament, such as verandahs to the viharas, and framings to the great window in the chaitya caves, as were always in good taste, and the purpose and meaning of which was at once seen. There is no instance of a Buddhist copying an exterior, as is here the case, or any building not a cave.

The similarity of this temple to that at Barolli also enables me, at least approximately, to determine its age; for I have made up my mind, for reasons which I cannot enter on here, that the former was erected in the eighth or ninth century after Christ. This probably was coeval. The sculpture, too, though executed in rather a coarser material, (fine hard freestone,) here is very similar in design and execution.

ELLORA.

I have put off speaking of Ellora to nearly the last, not only because it contains some of the most modern cave temples of India, but because it is the most complicated series I am acquainted with, containing examples of almost every kind, except, perhaps, the most ancient, and therefore demanding more knowledge of the subject to understand it, than any other series; and also, because, as being the best known in Europe and the one generally quoted for its unknown antiquity, I shall have to contend more with preconceived opinions than when speaking of the others. Its having been so often described, however, will enable me to be more concise and say less on the subject than I should otherwise have been obliged to do.

It is usual for travellers to be awe-struck on first approaching "this vast amphitheatre of rock-cut temples." It is, however, the principal defect of this style of building that it makes so little appearance outside. Some of the Vihara caves have fine fronts, but being either as a cliff as at Ajunta, or Karli, they bear much the same proportion to the rock as a window does to a house side, and therefore lose any appearance of size, or they are excavated on the sloping side of a hill as at Ellora, and can only be seen directly in front; the Viharas are never fine externally, and here less so than usual, owing to the sloping nature of the hill; and the Kylas is absolutely invisible from the exterior. Indeed, a man might ride along the whole front, and at a few hundred yards' distance, and, unless previously warned, never be aware that he was in their vicinity.

To convey to the European mind a still greater impression of their magnificence, it has been asserted more than once, that they are cut in hard red granite, whereas, the rock is the usual trap formation of this side of India, a sort of porphyritic greenstone or amygdaloid, I believe; but whatever it is, certainly as soft and as easily worked a material as could well be used for architectural purposes.

The amphitheatre of rocky hill in which they are situated cannot be less than two or three miles measured on the chord; and the caves are scattered over a distance about a mile and a half. Sir Charles

Mallet says, one mile from the Indra Subha to the Viswakarma in a direct line; this great space takes very much away from the effect when viewed as a whole; and it is only when in the courts of the caves, or when studying their details, that you are aware of their greatness or magnificence.

In describing these caves most travellers commence with the most northern group, the Jugganath Subha, and proceed to the most southern, the Viswakarma group; both Sir Charles Mallet and Colonel Sykes follow this plan, and the guides invariably take the traveller to the most northern first, so that if the notes are commenced on the first inspection, they almost certainly take this direction. Seely is almost the only exception I know to this rule, and he plunges at once "in medias res," and describes first the Kylas, and then the others indiscriminately.

The true way, however, to describe this series (which as far as I am aware no one has followed,) is to commence from the southern extremity, where the Buddhist group exists, and, consequently, the most ancient caves of the series, and the gradation is then easily perceived by which they passed into the Brahmanical, which, after rising to its glory in the Kylas and Doomar Lena, again for a short time passed into the half-Jaina group of the Jugganath Subha, and ended there.

I regret much that my notes on these caves are not more full than they are; but having read detailed descriptions by such men as Sir Charles Mallet, Colonel Sykes, Seely, Wales, &c., I thought nothing remained undescribed, and merely noted what bore directly on the subject of my researches; and the volumes that contain these descriptions being much too bulky to be carried about, it was not till too late that I discovered how much, particularly among the Buddhist temples, remains to be known, and described.

The whole series of Ellora consists of about thirty excavations, of which ten are Buddhistical, fourteen Brahmanical, and six belong, properly speaking, to neither of these sects, and they can scarcely be in strictness ascribed to the Jains, though savouring more of their religious tenets than of either Brahmanism or Buddhism.

Of the Buddhist group the principal cave is the so called Viswakarma, the only Chaitya cave of the series; it is neither so large as those at Karli or Salsette, being only forty-three feet wide internally, by eighty-three feet one inch in length, nor is it so rich in its details as the two later Chaityas at Ajunta. Still it has beauties of its own which render it highly interesting; its exterior court-yard (a square of about seventy feet with a handsome colonnade on three sides,) and the simple lines of the front form to my eye a more pleasing exterior than that of any of the others, at least at present, though it is impossible now to judge of what their effect may have been when their galleries and wooden decorations were complete.

It differs from all others in having what we would call a triple or Venetian window in the centre, which externally is certainly more pleasing than the great arch in the others; but that as I have suggested above was probably not seen from without, and internally, this cave is certainly worse lighted than the others; though in such a climate its gloom can scarcely be called a defect.

Internally the design of the temple is marked with considerable elegance and simplicity; the two pillars that support the gallery over the entrance are rich and handsome; the twenty-eight others are simple octagons, changing in one part to sixteen sides, and of great elegance.

The sculpture in the panels of the triforium belt disappointed me, but under the springing of each of the stone ribs of the roof is a corbel figure, alternately male and female, all the males having the snake hood, which the females have not.

In front of the daghopa is Buddha sitting with his feet down, with an attendant on each side, and over his head are a number of flying figures, only found in the most modern Buddhist caves, and savouring much more of Brahmanism than the pure worship of Sakya Muni; there is no trace of painting or stucco on the cave, though the side walls of the aisles being left rough, look as if that had been intended by the original excavators.

Though the form and ordinance of this temple are purely and correctly Buddhistical, the sculptures deviate strangely from the usual forms adopted by that sect; standing, for instance, in the court-yard, you do not see any figures of the deified, no cross-legged Buddha, or Bodhisatwá, except in a very subordinate position; and on the contrary, the sculptures generally consist of pairs of figures, male and female, as seen in Brahmanical temples, and in one group in no very decent attitude, the only instance I am aware of anything approaching to indecency in any temple of this sect; internally the same is the case; and it is indeed, too evident, that the pure religion of Buddha had deviated much from its primitive simplicity before this cave was excavated, and that it was already verging fast to that which succeeded it; a circumstance which alone would be sufficient to bring down its date to a very modern time; but the details of its architecture afford more certain means of comparison, and place it somewhere between the two most modern Chaityas at Ajunta; it may be as old as the one, or as modern as the other; but it cannot, I think, under any circumstances, be placed higher than the sixth or seventh century of our era, and I would not bring it down lower than the eighth or ninth.

There are numerous Viharas attached to this great cave, the principal of which is the great Dehrwarra, one of the largest excavations of the class that I know of; being about one hundred and ten feet by seventy, including the side recesses; it is, unfortunately for effect, very low, and its details are by no means to be compared to those of a similar age at Ajunta. It is probably of the same date as the Viswakarma; if any thing, more modern.

Close to the great cave is a small and very pretty Vihara, in which the sanctuary stands free, with a passage all round it, as in some of the Sivite caves further on; and the appearance of the warders on each side of its door would lead one rather to expect an image of Siva inside than the Buddha which actually occupies it. The details, however, of its architecture are the same as in the Viswakarma.

Communicating with this one, is a small square Vihara, the roof of which is supported by four pillars of the same detail as the Dookya-ghur, the cave next it on the north; but though surrounded by cells it has no sanctuary or images.

Higher up the hill than these are two others containing numerous cells, and one with a very handsome hall, the outer half of which has unfortunately tumbled in; enough, however, remains to show not only its plan, but all the details, which very much resemble those of the last group of Viharas at Ajunta.

In the sanctuaries of most of these caves are figures of Buddhas sitting with their feet down. On each side of the image in the principal one, are nine figures of Buddhas, or rather Bodhisatwas, seated cross-legged, and below them three and three figures, some cross-legged, and others standing, probably devotees, and one of them a woman.

Neither of these caves have been entirely finished.

There is still another group of these small Viharas, called the Chumarwarra, or, (if I understand correctly,) the Chumars' (or shoemakers') quarter. The first is square, with twelve pillars on the same plan as those at Ajunta, though the detail is similar to the Viswakarma. There are cells, and in the sanctuary Buddha sitting with the feet down; it never has been finished, and is now much ruined.

The second is similar in plan, though the pillars are of the cushion form of Elephanta and the Dehrwarra, but the capitals are much better formed, than in the last example, and more ornamented; the lateral galleries here contain figures of Buddha, all like the one in the sanctuary sitting with their feet down, and there are only two cells on each side of the sanctuary.

The last is a small plain Vihara with cells, but without pillars, and much ruined.

The whole of the caves in this group resemble one another so much in detail and execution, that I am unable to make out any succession among them, and it is probable that they were all excavated within the same century as the Viswakarma.

The next three temples I have to describe are particularly interesting to the antiquarian, as pointing out the successive steps by which the Buddhistical caves merged into Brahmanism. As they have been so often described, I need not repeat the description here, but assume that their form and detail are known.

The first is the Do Tal, or Dookya Ghur, a Buddhist Vihara of two stories; most of its details are so similar to those above described, that it may be assumed to be without doubt of the same age; it is strictly Buddhistic in all its details, and shows no more tendency towards Brahmanism than what I pointed out in speaking of Viswakarma. It apparently was intended to have three stories, but has been left unfinished.

The next, or Teen Tal, is very similar to the last in arrangement and detail, and its sculptures are all Buddhistical, though deviating so far from the usual simplicity of that style, as almost to justify the Brahmans in appropriating them as they have done.

The third, the Dasavatar, is another two-storied cave, very similar in all its architecture and details to the two preceding, but the sculptures are all Brahmanical. At first, I assumed, that the excavation had been made by the Buddhists, and appropriated and finished by their successors. This may be true to a certain extent, but on a more careful examination I am more inclined to think we owe it entirely to the Brahmans. It it evidently the earliest Brahmanical temple here, and it is natural to suppose that when the Sivites first attempted to rival their antagonists in cave temples, they should follow the only models that existed, merely appropriating it to their own worship. The circumstance, however, that makes me most incline to this opinion, is the existence of a pseudo-structural Mantapa, or shrine of Nundi, in the court-yard; this evidently must have been a part of the original design, or the rock would not have been left here for it, and it is a model of the usual structural building found in Sivite temples in different parts of India. And as I pointed out in speaking of the Dhumnar caves, this is a piece of bad grammar the Buddhists never were guilty of; their excavations always are caves, whilst the characteristic of Brahmanical excavation is to copy their structural buildings, a system which rose to its height in the Kylas, which is the next I shall have to describe.

After the successful attempt at a small rock-cut model of one of their own temples, it is not wonderful that the Brahmans should attempt something of the same class on a larger scale, though some powerful motive must have existed to induce them to attempt any thing so splendid as the Kylas.

In it there is no trace of the forms or ordinances of the caves I have just been describing; every thing is Brahmanical, every thing is copied from structural buildings; and had it been cut out of a rock on a plain, (its proper situation,) no stranger would have suspected that it was a Monolith, without at least, a most careful examination of its structure.

If, as I suppose was the case, it was undertaken to mark the triumph of the Sivites over the Buddhist faith, it was a noble idea; and whatever faults may be inherent in the design, we owe to it not only the most splendid excavation in India, but we are also fortunate in possessing a record of the architecture of its date in so imperishable a form, and which may hereafter help us to make important historical deductions.

The greatest fault inherent in the design is the situation in which the Kylas stands, being literally, as at Dhumnar, a temple standing in a pit. From this circumstance, the gateway, or gopura, and screen in front, entirely hide the temple from view outside, and when in the interior court the space is so confined, that the spectator can never get to a sufficient distance to get a good general view, and look what way he will he has always the perpendicular scarp of the pit, higher than the temple itself.

When I first approached the Kylas, it was after a long journey, during the course of which I had visited almost all the Hindú remains between Jaganath on the shores of the Bay of Bengal, and Mount Abu on the borders of the western desert; and I had acquired such familiarity with the style and details of Hindú architecture, that I felt convinced I should at once be able to synchronize this wonder of Ellora with some of the temples I had seen, and even perhaps to affix a date to it. The first glance however undeceived me, as the style was totally different from any thing I had seen, and one might as soon attempt to fix the date of a Gothic cathedral, from having acquired an intimate knowledge of the classic styles. Unlike the temple at Dhumnar, which is an exact copy of the structural buildings in its neighbourhood, this belongs to a southern type, and that type I had not then had an opportunity of seeing or examining; and as I have often said, there are no drawings extant of Indian buildings which will enable an antiquarian to make the comparison without personal inspection.

It was not till the spring of the present year that I was able to complete my survey of Hindú architecture by a tour in the Carnatic, and it was then at Tanjore and Chillumbrum that I found the type I was looking for. It would perhaps be going too far to assert that the builders of the great pagoda at Tanjore were the excavators of the Kylas; and it would certainly take up more time and space than I can afford here to attempt to prove it; but so strong is the evidence, not only from the similarity of styles but also from history, (I should rather say tradition,) that I have no doubt in my own mind, that the Chola, or at least, some of the Karnata Rajas were the excavators of this temple, and the restorers of Sivite worship in the Dekkan; my own impression is, that we must ascribe this to either Raja Rajendra or Keri Kala Cholan, and that consequently the date given by Meer Ali Khan to Sir Charles Mallet is very near the truth, if applied to this excavation, at least, and that it was made in the first half of the ninth century of our era.

The external gateway is exactly one of the gopuras which adorn all the temples of the south, and are unknown in the north; whether it had ever the pyramidical top with which all these are adorned it is not very easy now to determine. I am inclined to think it had, but if so, it would be of brick, as all those are, though their base is universally of granite, to the height at which this one of the Kylas remains.

The colonnade which surrounds the area in which the temple stands, is of course more modern than the temple itself; probably considerably so, as the style is different, and resembles more the northern style than any thing in the temple itself, so much so indeed, that it would almost seem as if the architects had reverted to the familiar types of the caves previously described, after the retirement of their southern friends.

Of a still more modern date is the beautiful temple of Lanka in the northern scarp of the rock, to which I shall revert presently, and to a later date than even this would I ascribe the two-arched Buddhist-looking excavation on each side of the entrance, one of which, that of the north, is only commenced, that on the south nearly finished. It is possible they may have been placed there with the idea of conciliating the Buddhists by the first designers of the temple, but I consider it as much more probable that they have been added at some time, when, for a short interval, the Buddhists may have had the upper hand, and consequently possession of the temple.

I should also mention, that the Vimana itself is the only thing here of a purely southern type, its adjuncts are less so; and the caves, both on the north and south sides, have much more affinity with the northern styles, than with those found on the south of the Kistna.

The next six caves proceeding north, have been so often and so well described, that I may be excused saying much about them; they are usually called the Rameswara, Neelcant, Teeli ka kanah, Kumarwarra, and the two Chendwassas.

They are all very much on the same plan, and all singularly like small Buddhist Viharas at first sight, so much so, that after being convinced they were Brahmanical, I still clung to the idea that they must be appropriations; but this idea must be abandoned, for they are all without cells, and there are arrangements about them never seen in Viharas; and had they been once used by the Buddhists it would have been impossible, in a rock temple, to obliterate the marks of their former destination. Imitations they certainly are, and this is perhaps all that can be said of them; though it is difficult to understand why the Brahmans should have imitated the Buddhists, unless it was (as before suggested) to conciliate the followers of the latter religion, by allowing them to worship the new gods in rock-cut temples, similar to those in which their fathers had worshipped before them.

The architecture of all these temples is of a northern type, and resembles, with some variation, details found in the caves to the south of the Kylas, and at Ajunta, though differing in some respects to suit the two different religions to which they are dedicated.

The Rameswara is the most complete, and its sculpture the best of any temple here, though much in the same style as those surrounding the Kylas.

The most northern of the two Chendwassas is the only Vaishnava temple here, and at the same time the one that looks most like an appropriation, for it has cells, and the sculpture seems to have been interpolated on the original design. The sculpture, however, is so bad that the whole may belong to an age very much more modern than the others.

The next to be described is the Doomar Lena[1], the finest and largest Brahmanical cave excavation here. From its plan and details, there can be no doubt that it was as purely Brahmanical as the Kylas. The plan exactly resembles the Chaöri, or nuptial hall, such as those in front of the great temple at Barolli, and also the one in the fort at

[1] Plate No. 4.

Kumulmair; and if I am correct in translating Chaöri as nuptial hall, as Tod does, the appellation Doomar Lena here given, is the correct one, and not merely a trivial name, derived from one of the sculptured groups, as usually supposed. Indeed, had that been the case, they would hardly have used the Pali word Lena. The only difference between this, and the structural Chaöris, is that here the temple or vimana is inclosed in the cave, while at Barolli, and elsewhere, the Chaöri stands in front of the temple. The same thing occurs in Buddhist architecture, for in all Buddhist countries we find the daghopa outside, and near the temple: in the caves it is placed inside.

Though the architecture of this cave is finished, the sculpture does not seem so complete as at Elephanta, a cave which this one singularly resembles in every respect, both of size, plan, and detail; this, however, is the largest, being a hundred and fifty feet each way, while the other is only a hundred and thirty, and its details are somewhat better finished; though the pillars are so much alike, that it requires drawings made on the spot to detect the difference between them[1].

The sculptures, too, seem intended to have been nearly the same, and on the side of the entrance we find the same figure of Buddha, or, as the people call him here, Jam Dhurm, the Dharma Raja, which puzzles the antiquarian at Elephanta. I can only ascribe his presence to the same system of conciliation which induced the Brahmans to go out of their way to dig these caves at all.

This temple, with the one at Elephanta, if I am correct in the views I have stated above, must have been excavated in the tenth century of our era, a date which I do not think can possibly be far from the truth.

In a nullah above this are several small caves, containing Trimurti busts, and one also exists near the Kylas. They are not remarkable for any thing else, and what I have to say of the busts in question had better be deferred till I come to speak of Elephanta.

There are two caves which I have passed over in the above enumeration, so as not to break the chronological sequence in my description. The first, the Ravana ka Kaie, (Ashes of Ravana,) is situated between the Teen Tal and Das Avatar, but lower down in the hill, and has few points of similarity with those on each side of it. It is a purely Brahmanical cave of a florid style of architecture. In form the pillars resemble a good deal those that surround the court-yard of the Viswakarma, though more ornamented, and it is here that first appears the vase and falling leaf, so common, afterwards, in the temples of

[1] Plate No. 9.

northern India. The sculpture is good, and similar to that of the Rameswara in many respects. I have however described it by itself, as there is no cave in Ellora whose relative date I found so difficult to determine. It may possibly belong to the position it holds locally in the series, and would be thus the earliest Brahmanical cave here, and the similarity of its pillars to those of the Viswakarma, rather favour this supposition; but its floridness, the style of sculpture, and the general disposition of the cave, incline me to place it much later, or, as here described, after the Doomar Lena.

The other cave is called Lanka, and is situated above the colonnade in the northern scarp of the Kylas; from its position evidently executed subsequently to the great temple, and, from its design, I should think not less than one or two centuries later. Its details all belong to the northern styles, and are bold and good; indeed, as a specimen of cave architecture, I consider it the finest and best designed in the whole series. The pillars, which would be clumsy and heavy in a structural building, are elegant and appropriate when viewed in conjunction with the mass of rock they support. There are very few sculptures, and these are not remarkable either for execution or design. Indeed the cave does not seem to have been entirely finished, or every compartment would, without doubt, have contained some group of sculpture.

The next caves to be described are the Indra Subha group, consisting of four principal caves, and several smaller ones.

In their architecture they differ very considerably from those already described, being generally more ornate, the pillars shorter and more massive, and a species of leaf falling over a vase being here introduced, which does not occur in any of the earlier examples; though something of the kind is seen as above mentioned, in the Ravana ka Kaie, and in the Lanka; indeed the style of the last-named cave so completely resembles that of the Indra Subha, that I have no hesitation in placing them nearly in the same age, though it would be difficult to say which is the more modern.

The sculptures to this group have hitherto proved a stumbling-block to antiquaries, and no fixed opinion seems to have been arrived at regarding them. Buddhist they certainly are not, or at all events of so degenerate a type as scarce to deserve that name; nor are they Brahmanical; and though they certainly resemble Jaina sculpture more than any other, I do not think they can be correctly ascribed to that sect either, at least as we now know it. In no place in these caves do the twenty-four thirthankars appear, nor have the cross-legged figures the symbols which almost invariably accompany these worthies, and are the only means of distinguishing one from another. If, however, I am correct in supposing Jainism to be a sort of compromise between the other two religions, which did not acquire its present form and consistency till after the downfall of the Buddhists, when they were joined by most of that sect who had not embraced the dominant religion, these caves are doubly interesting as showing us the religion in a state of transition from one set of tenets to another.

Be this as it may, I have little doubt that they are the last caves executed here, and I do not think their date can be carried higher than the eleventh or twelfth century of our era. Indeed, from a similarity in some of the details, I would feel almost inclined to ascribe them to Raja Indra Dyumna, who plays so important a part here, and in the building of the famous Jaganatha Pagoda, in Orissa, in the twelfth century; but it would require more knowledge and labour than I can at present apply to the subject, to make out whether this be really the case or not[1].

There is one singularity in these caves that I am unable to explain, which is the form of the pseudo-structural temple in the court yard, in front of the Indra Subha. Like the Kylas, it seems to have come from the south, while the details all round it belong to the northern types; and though its age would by no means interfere with the date given above, its appearance here is singular, and its detail still more so. The difficulty will perhaps only be solved by a more attentive examination of the structural temples of the Dekkan than I have been able to make.

ELEPHANTA.

The great cave at Elephanta has been described so well, and in such detail, by Mr. Erskine, in the Transactions of the Bombay Literary Society, that I may be excused saying much about it.

The rock here is much harder than at Ellora, and all the details are consequently cut with more precision, and better preserved, than in the caves there; but neither the outline nor general design are better than in the sculpture of the Hindu series there.

The great cave, as I said before, is of the form now called a Chaori, and differs from the one at Ellora only in the position of the Ling chapel, or sanctuary; and the great Trimurti bust, which may have been

[1] See Introduction to Wilson's Catalogue of Mackenzie's MSS., p. cvi.; also, Asiatic Researches, vol. xv., p. 316; and Dr. Buchanan Hamilton's Statistics of Bagulpur, p. 23.

intended, in the Doomar Lena, for the space opposite the entrance, is there left blank, though the position of the sanctuary renders this improbable. The great bust is now generally allowed to be of Siva alone, and I will not add anything to the discussion, further than by mentioning that at Barolli there is a bust of large dimensions, and almost exactly similar to this; but being cut in fine hard stone, all that remains of it is more easily distinguishable than here. The centre face, however, is unfortunately entirely defaced, but that on its right has a chaplet of skulls, and the "frontlet eye" open, and an angry and animated expression of countenance. The face on the left has also the frontlet eye distinctly marked, but as no eyeball is shown, I presume it is meant to be represented as shut; but what adds particular interest to this bust is, that over it, on the same stone, are full-length statues of Brahma and Vishnu, the former over the right face, with his three (query four?) faces, and his Vahana, the goose, the latter as usually represented, with his four arms, and the gadhi, chakra, &c., circumstances which quite put to rest the idea of the bust itself representing the three persons of the Trinity, nor can I concur with Colonel Sykes in supposing the left face to be Parvati. The three I believe to be Siva, as creator, preserver, and destroyer; an assumption of the attributes of the other two ascribed to him by his votaries when his worship became dominant.

In a ravine running from the great cave across the island, there are two other caves, similar in plan to those situated between the Kylas and Doomar Lena, at Ellora. These unfortunately, however, are so much injured by the falling of the rock and the damp, that it is impossible to make out more than their dedication to Siva, and a general similarity to those of Ellora, with which I have no doubt they are cotemporary: indeed there is a degree of similarity between the two series which is singular in structures so distant, and which can only be accounted for by their being undertaken at the same time, and probably under the same direction.

I could find no trace of Buddhism in the whole island, and these, therefore, are perhaps singular, as being the only purely Brahmanical series in the north of India; for though those at Joyghesir and Montpezir are likewise purely Hindu, and apparently of the same age as these, they are situated in the same island, and so nearly in the vicinity of the great Buddhist series of Kannari, that the motive before ascribed, as inducing the Brahmans to become cave diggers, applies to them.

MAHAVELLIPORE.

One only series remains now to be described, and which, though not so magnificent or extensive as some of those which have already passed under review, still possesses peculiarities and distinctive features, which render it scarce less interesting to the artist or the antiquary.

Like Ellora, however, it has been so often described by Europeans, that little remains to be added to what has been already published on the subject, first by Messrs. Chambers and Goldingham in the Asiatic Researches, and afterwards, with more precision, by Mr. Babington, in the Transactions of the Royal Asiatic Society. The notices of Bishop Heber and Mrs. Graham are also interesting, though not bearing on the present subject of inquiry.

Between Covelong and Sadras, a long sandy ridge extends near forty miles, bounded on the east by the sea, and on the west by a salt-water lagoon, now dry for the greater part of the year. Towards the southern extremity of this ridge, a number of masses of granite rock protrude through the surface, so numerous and large in one spot as to form a hill about a mile in length, with half that breadth, and rising to the height of about a hundred or a hundred and fifty feet; and it is in this hill that the principal antiquities are situated, consisting of some half-dozen of caves in various states of progress, one pseudo-structural temple, and the famous bas-reliefs. About half a mile to the south of this, are the five raths, and on the rock jutting into the sea, due east from the centre of the hill, the famous structural temple, known as the remaining one of the seven pagodas, from which the place takes its European name.

The most completely finished cave here, (for none is entirely so,) is the small one in the ravine, figured in Babington's ninth plate. It is architecturally complete, though its sculpture is not quite finished. The finest cave, however, is the one containing the fine bas-relief of Kali killing Mahaasura, (see plate 4 in Babington's description) by far the finest piece of sculpture here, and equal to anything at Ellora. The frontispiece of this cave, however, is merely blocked out, and its cells are unfinished. Like the others it is small when compared with the northern caves, being only thirty-two feet ten inches, by fifteen feet six inches, in the interior, exclusive of the three cells; the centre one of which is occupied by Siva sitting on Nandi, with Parvati and Sobramuni, and above them Brahma and Vishnu. In form and detail this cave may be compared to the Rameswar at Ellora, or perhaps rather to number seven at Ajunta. It cannot, however, be so old as either of them, as the architecture is poorer, leaner, and its details resemble much more those used in structural buildings of a more modern date than the massive style of cave architecture that distinguishes these specimens[1]. That it is a copy from these caves can scarcely I think be doubted, but not one of the same age.

Immediately above this cave, and apparently intended to form part of the design, is the base of a structural vimana of the same age and style; the part remaining is of granite, and it probably never was finished, or if the pyramid was built of brick, as is the universal custom in the south, it probably has fallen down. This is the only instance I am aware of such an adjunct, though they may have been common in Brahmanical caves.

Opposite the front of this cave, at the distance of a few yards, the workmen have commenced to hew a temple out of an immense block that stands there; its form is scarcely distinguishable, but it is interesting as showing the mode in which the workmen set about an undertaking of this sort, which was simply to divide the rock into squares of about twelve and eighteen inches, by channels two and three inches deep, and then to split off the remaining mass, which the tendency of granite to exfoliate easily enabled them to do.

There is another pseudo-structural temple of nearly the same size and design as this one was intended to be, at the northern end of the hill, and which is nearly, though not quite, finished.

Immediately behind the present village temple, and about half way between the two caves above-mentioned, is the great bas-relief so often figured, though never so well as by Mr. Babington, in the paper above referred to. The elephants are good, and so are many of the figures, particularly the ascetic; but the whole wants unity of design and purpose, and is inferior in every respect to the Kali sculpture in the cave above, to many of those at Ellora, and to all the sculptures of Elephanta. The rock, too, has not been smoothed away between the figures, which gives the whole an appearance of not being finished, and isolates the figures and groups in a very disagreeable manner.

Adjoining is an unfinished excavation very like (in plan), to the trimurti cave near the Kylas, and a little further to the south the other large bas-relief, which, though of the same age, is of inferior execution to the great one.

The five raths are situated about a mile south of the hill in the direction of its axis, and though small, and of course unfinished, (like everything else here,) are as pleasing examples of their style as any I

[1] Plate No. 10.

know. They possess an immense advantage over the pseudo-structural temples of the north; for being cut out of detached masses of granite, they stand alone in the sand, and are in every respect so like structural buildings, that it requires some examination to convince one's self they are not so. They have also the advantage in material, being cut from a fine, bold-grained granite, of a reddish tinge. It has, however, a tendency to split, which the trap of the north has not, and exfoliates when long exposed to the weather.

Daniell's views of these temples, and the various descriptions extant, have rendered them so familiar to the public that I need not say more regarding them here; though I much wish that the elaborate architectural drawings made of them for Colonel Mackenzie could be given to the public, as they would afford juster notions of what Indian antiquities really are, than any thing that has yet been published.

I could not find in any of the temples or sculptures here the smallest trace of Buddhist worship. Every where Siva appears as the presiding deity, though with a singularly liberal allowance of Vishnuism. In the cave first mentioned so completely is this the case, that it might almost be called Vaishnava; and in the second the pendant to the Kali bas-relief is a Vishnu reposing on the Ses Seja; and in the raths the only cell that is occupied is occupied by Lakshmi, though this arises, I believe, from the unfinished state of the others; for they were certainly intended to be dedicated to Siva. It has been doubted to whom the temple on the shore is dedicated; and its sculptures, those at least on the walls, have been so corroded by the sea air, that they cannot well be made out; and though Siva and Parvati appear on two separate bas-reliefs, occupying the principal places, they may not be integral, and the large figure drawn by Babington, plate twelve, is Vishnu on the Ses Seja, extremely similar to the one in the Kali cave, while the broken Sthamba in the central apartment may or may not be a Lingam, though I myself have little doubt that it is, and that the temple was Sivite.

One of the most singular characteristics of this series of caves is that they are all of one age, and probably the work of one prince, who has carried on the works simultaneously, but from some cause or other has been unable to complete even one of them; had one been finished, or had there been any gradation of style or workmanship, some chronological arrangement might easily have been traced; but nothing of the sort exists, at least among the monoliths, and the temple on the shore does not fall strictly within my present limits, though I may mention that its age does not differ materially from that of the rest.

If the north owe its Kylas to the Chola mandalam, which I believe it certainly does, the south as certainly owes these Monoliths to the Dekkan. There is nothing here of which the prototype cannot be traced in the caves of the north. In plan and design they resemble the Hindu series at Ellora, though many of their details are only to be found at Ajunta and Salsette; and it cannot be supposed that two people, unless copying from one another, could have invented the same details in so short a period as could have elapsed between the excavating of these, and those of the northern caves; and besides, no one, I believe, will doubt, after what has been said above, that cave architecture is indigenous in the north, while these are the only specimens found in the south.

Passing by those traditions which refer to Maha Bali and the Gods, which at all events have no reference to anything now existing here, there are two which bear an appearance of great probability. The first mentioned by Mr. Goldingham, vol. v., Trans. A.S., p. 74, thus:

"A northern prince, (perhaps one of the conquerors,) about one thousand years ago, was desirous of having a great work executed, but the Hindu sculptors and masons refused to execute it on the terms he offered. Attempting force, they (in number about four thousand,) fled with their effects from his country, hither, where they resided four or five years, and in this interval executed these magnificent works. The prince at length discovering them, prevailed on them to return, which they did, leaving the works unfinished as they appear at present."

The second is from the Mackenzie MSS., as abstracted by Mr. Taylor, in the Madras Journal, No. 20, p. 65.

"In the Cali Yug, Singhama Nayadu, the Zemindar of the Vellugotivaru race, seemed to have ruled here. In that time, during a famine, many artificers resorted hither, and wrought on the mountain a great variety of works during two or three years."

Who this Singhama was appears from another MS. in the same collection, (M. J. No. 19, p. 373,) where, speaking of this race, it is said, "Vennama Nayadu became head of his race. His son was Yiradacha N., who with his cousin were successful in their incursions against neighbouring places, extending to Canchi and to the Pandya kings. The Mussulmans are also mentioned as beaten in defence of another chieftain. The son of Vennama, named Singhama Nayadu, became the head of this race."

The thousand years of the first quotation I look upon as the usual Hindu synonym for "some time ago," while the allusion to foreign conquerors seems to point to the only event I am aware of that would give probability to the tradition, namely, the invasion of Deoghur by Alla-uddín, in the end of the thirteenth century; a supposition rendered probable by the extracts from the Mackenzie manuscripts; for though no date is there given for Singhama's reign, it appears in the context that his grand-uncle or great-grand-uncle, was engaged in the revolution that placed Pratapa Rudra on the Ganapati throne, A.D. 1167, and he therefore flourished in the thirteenth century, probably towards the end of it. The allusion to the Mahomedan in this extract also renders this still more likely, as before Alla-uddín they scarcely meddled in the affairs of the south.

Though this evidence appears tolerably conclusive, I should not be inclined to rely upon it were it not corroborated by the internal evidence of the caves themselves. But altogether I fear five centuries and a half is all the antiquity we can allow to these boasted monuments of primeval times.

Singhama's death in the field, before the fort of Jalli Palli, is still more probably the cause of the sudden interruption of the works, than the reconciliation of the workmen with their northern master; it being entirely a fancy of his own, and neither indigénous in the country, nor a part of the religion of the people, it is not probable that his successor would continue the follies of his parent.

There is one other means of fixing approximately the date of these temples, to which I have not alluded, and on which I am incapable of forming an opinion; I mean the date of the characters inscribed on the large rath over the figures there. Their form, and Mr. Babington's being able to translate them, does not say much for their antiquity, though their general illegibility does, I confess, argue a higher antiquity than I have ascribed to the buildings.

Had any one done for the Alphabets of the south what Mr. Prinsep did for those of the north, the question would be easily determined, but till that is done, I fear this mode of proof is scarcely available.

In concluding this paper I would wish to add a few words on the present state of the caves, and on the means that might (and I now hope will,) be taken to preserve them from further injury before it is too late.

Those of Cuttack are, as I mentioned above, inhabited by Hindú Fakírs, but as they are not used as places of worship, or esteemed sacred by the inhabitants of the country, an order from the magistrate would, I conceive, be sufficient to dislodge them, and without interfering with any religious feelings of the people, which the Government are justly so careful of offending. If this were done very little trouble or expense would be required to remove the mud walls and rubbish they have accumulated, and thus restore to view these very interesting monuments.

Unless, however, it is intended to make and publish accurate drawings of the series, and to take some measures for their protection in future, it is scarcely to be wished that this should be done; for there is little doubt, judging from what has happened in other places, that a few pic-nic parties from Cuttack or Puri, and the destructive pilfering of a few would-be antiquarians, would do more harm in a few years, than has been done by their present occupants in centuries.

The caves of Ellora, Salsette, Junir, &c., are entirely deserted as places of worship, and therefore easily accessible to all Europeans. Their stucco and painting have however almost entirely disappeared, but their sculptures are not so easily broken, and are on too large a scale to tempt the cupidity of most collectors.

The cave at Elephanta being situated so near Bombay, was more exposed to injury than any of the others, and much was done, till Government at length appointed an invalid serjeant to look after and protect it; since that time it has been tolerably well cared for.

The great cave at Karli is now, strangely enough, taken possession of by the Brahmans, and considered a temple of Mahadeva. How far, therefore, interference with it would be practicable I do not know; access, however, is allowed to any strangers, and there are no paintings or sculptures which are likely to be injured by its present occupants, or even by English tourists.

The only series, therefore, that demands immediate attention is that of Ajunta; the caves there are entirely deserted by the natives, and are only visited by Europeans.

As I mentioned above they still retain the greater portion of their original paintings, but that is fast disappearing, and a traveller who would now visit them, will miss much that I saw a few years ago.

It is sad to think that after standing so many years an exposure to so destructive a climate, after escaping the bigotry of the Moslem, and the rough usage of the robber Bheel, they should be fast perishing from the meddling curiosity of the Europeans who now visit them. But such is unfortunately the case; for few come away without picking off one or two of the heads he thinks most beautiful or interesting, and as most of them are reduced to powder before they reach their destination, they are lost to the world for ever. The only instance of this I can refer to in print, is in the Journal of the Asiatic Society of Bengal, vol. v., p. 561, where it is stated, that Dr. Bird peeled four figures off the Zodiac in cave No. 17, and this is unfortunately not the only instance that has fallen under my observation.

I have now brought to a conclusion the remarks I had to make on the Cave Temples of India, which have extended to a much greater length than I supposed they would do when I originally undertook the task of compiling them. The number of objects, however, to be described is so great, that I have found it impossible to compress into shorter limits the foregoing descriptions, with the few remarks that were necessary to render the subject intelligible. Indeed, I am afraid that I am equally open to the opposite accusation of abruptness and obscurity from attempting too great conciseness; but I must be allowed to plead as an apology for this fault, as well as for the want of polish of style that pervades my descriptions, that in almost every instance, I have copied word for word in this paper the notes I made on the spot and in the caves themselves. By a little amplification and attention to style it would have been easy to have rendered the paper much more readable, but this would have added to its length, which is already too great; and besides, might, in describing objects so long after they were visited, have rendered my descriptions less correct, and thus have taken from them the only merit to which they can fairly pretend. I may also add, that when this paper was first written, it was my intention to have published at the same time, in a folio form, some eighteen or twenty of my sketches of the caves and temples described in the text, which, when taken with the illustrations now given, would, I conceive, have added much to the interest of the subject, besides supplying many of the deficiencies of the descriptions, of which no one is more fully aware that I am.

I regret, however, to say, that I have not as yet been able to find any publisher willing to undertake the publication on satisfactory terms, nor has the project met with sufficient encouragement in any quarter to which I have hitherto referred it, to induce me to undertake the risk and annoyance of bringing it out myself and on my own account; I am not, however, without hope that this may still be accomplished.

Since the foregoing paper was read, a Memorial was presented by the Council of this Society to the Court of Directors on the subject of these caves, to which I am happy to hear they have responded; and orders have, I believe, been forwarded to the different Presidencies to employ competent persons to draw and copy the antiquities and paintings in each district, and thus we may at last hope to have these caves illustrated in a manner worthy of their magnificence and great historical interest. I only hope the subject will not now be allowed to drop till every monument of ancient India has been thoroughly examined and detailed, and we may thus escape the hitherto too well merited reproach of having so long possessed that noble country, and done so little to illustrate its history or antiquities.

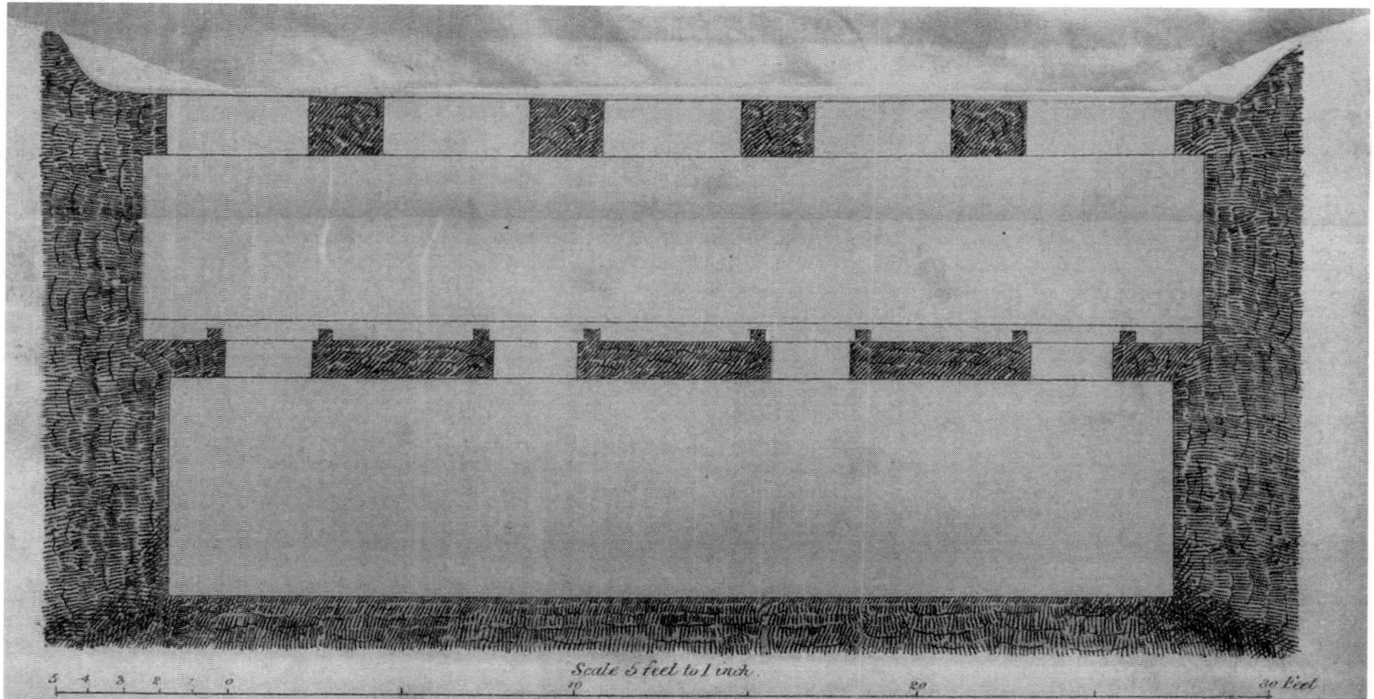

GANESA GUMPHA OR GUREHA UDYAGIRI.

Pl. 2.

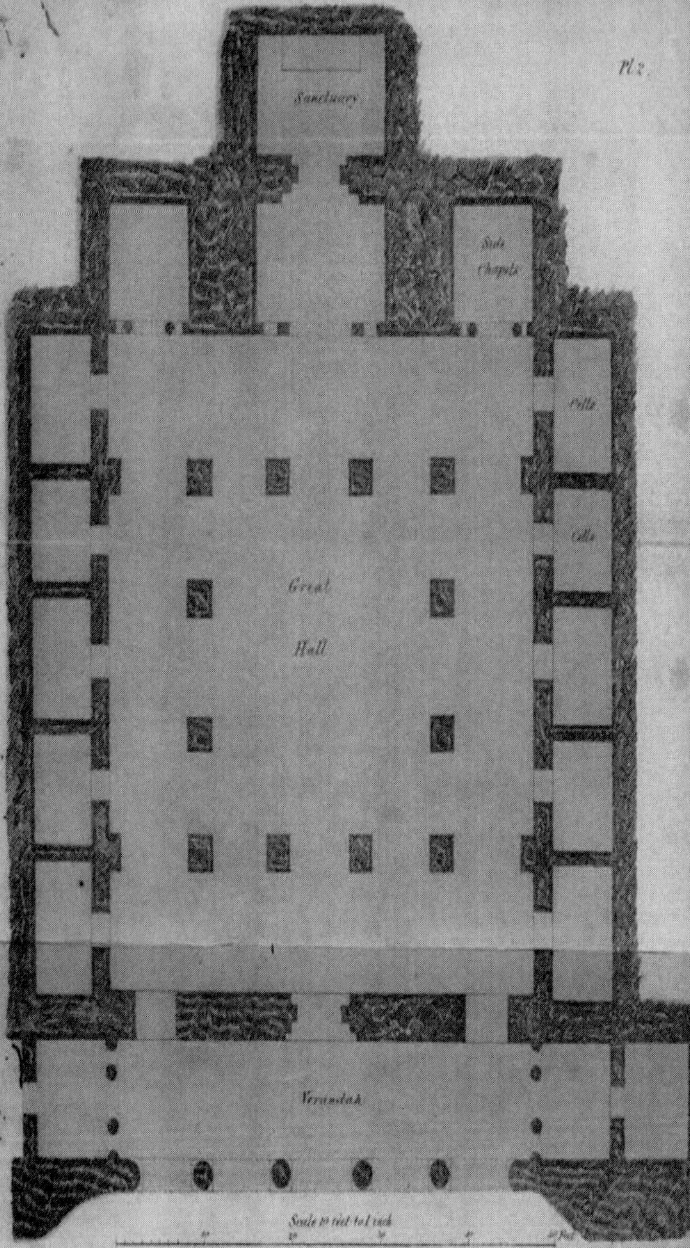

PLAN OF VIHARA CAVE No. 2 AT AJUNTA

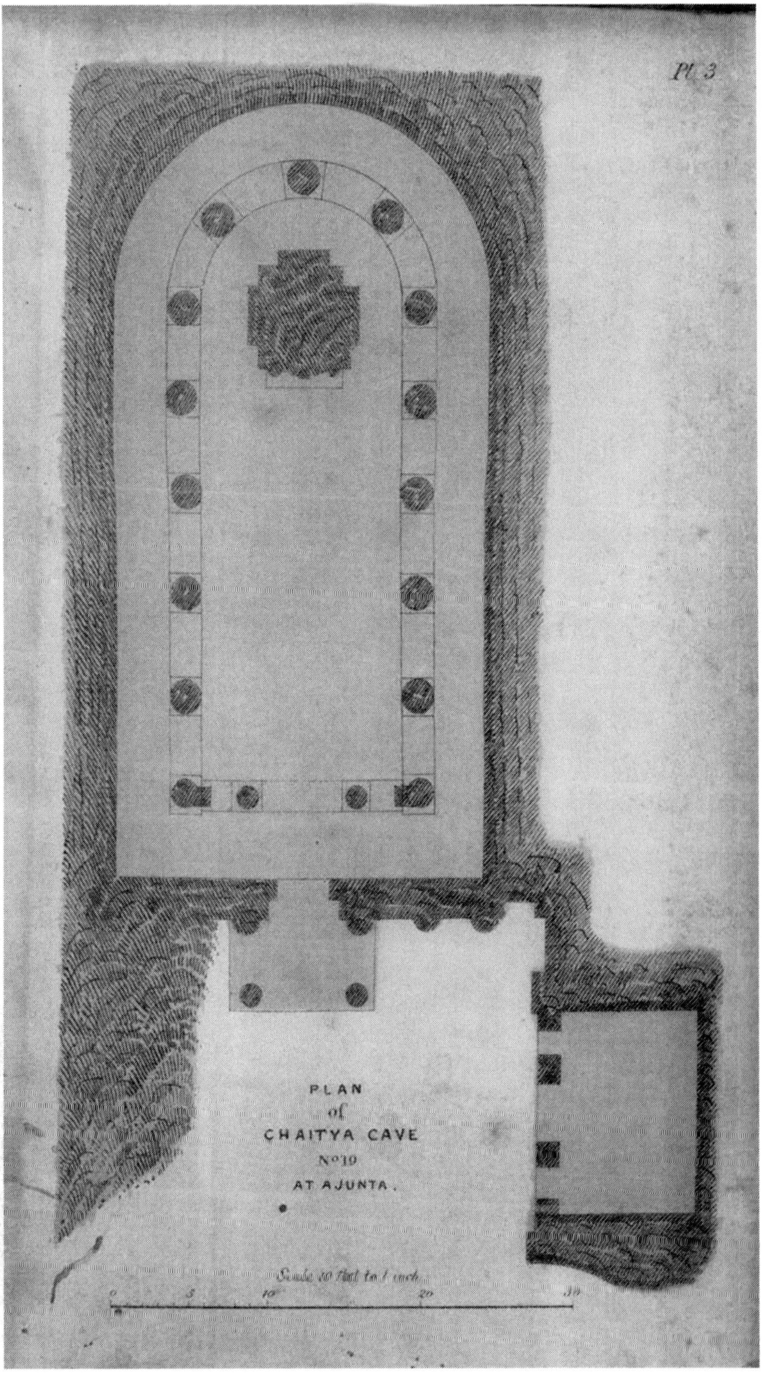
Pl. 3
PLAN
of
CHAITYA CAVE
No 19
AT AJUNTA.
Scale 10 feet to 1 inch.
0 5 10 20 30

Pl. 4.

Scale 25 Feet to 1 Inch.

DOOMAR LENA, ELLORA

Pl. 5.

PILLAR AND WINDOW IN CAVE No. 11. AT AJUNTA.

Pl. 6.

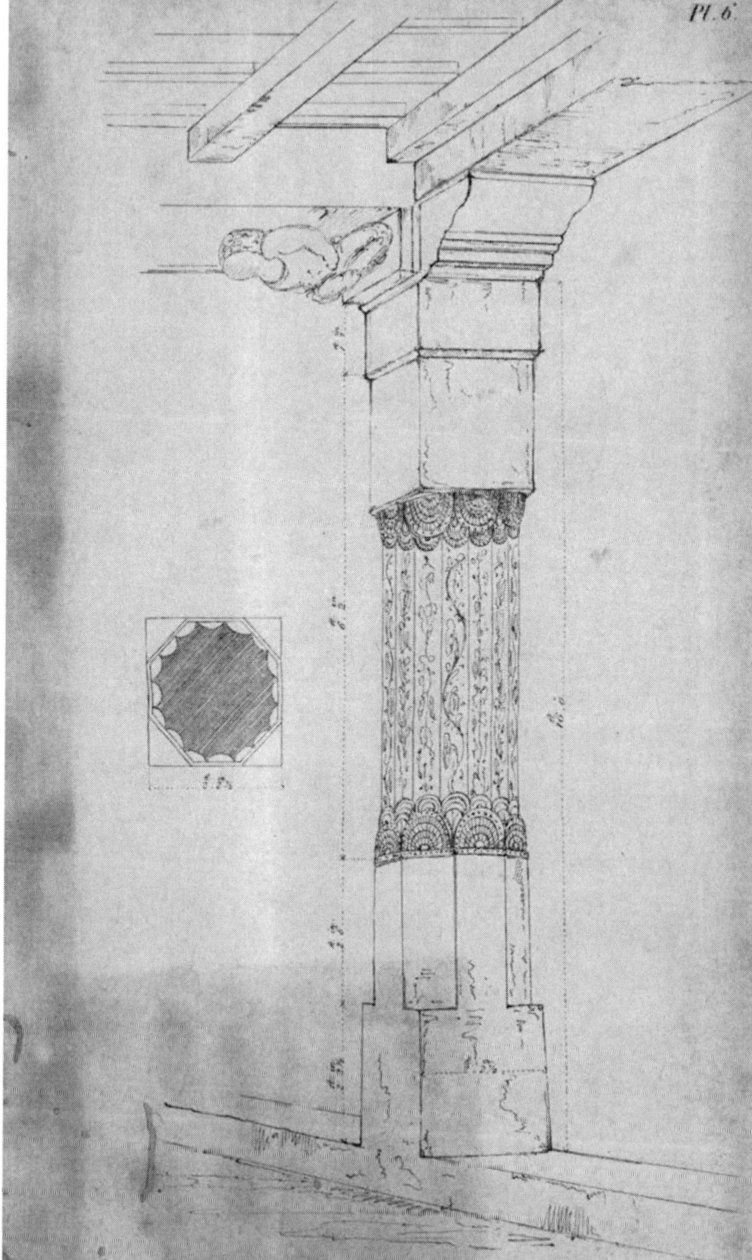

PILLAR IN CAVE Nº 17. AT AJUNTA.

Pl. 7.

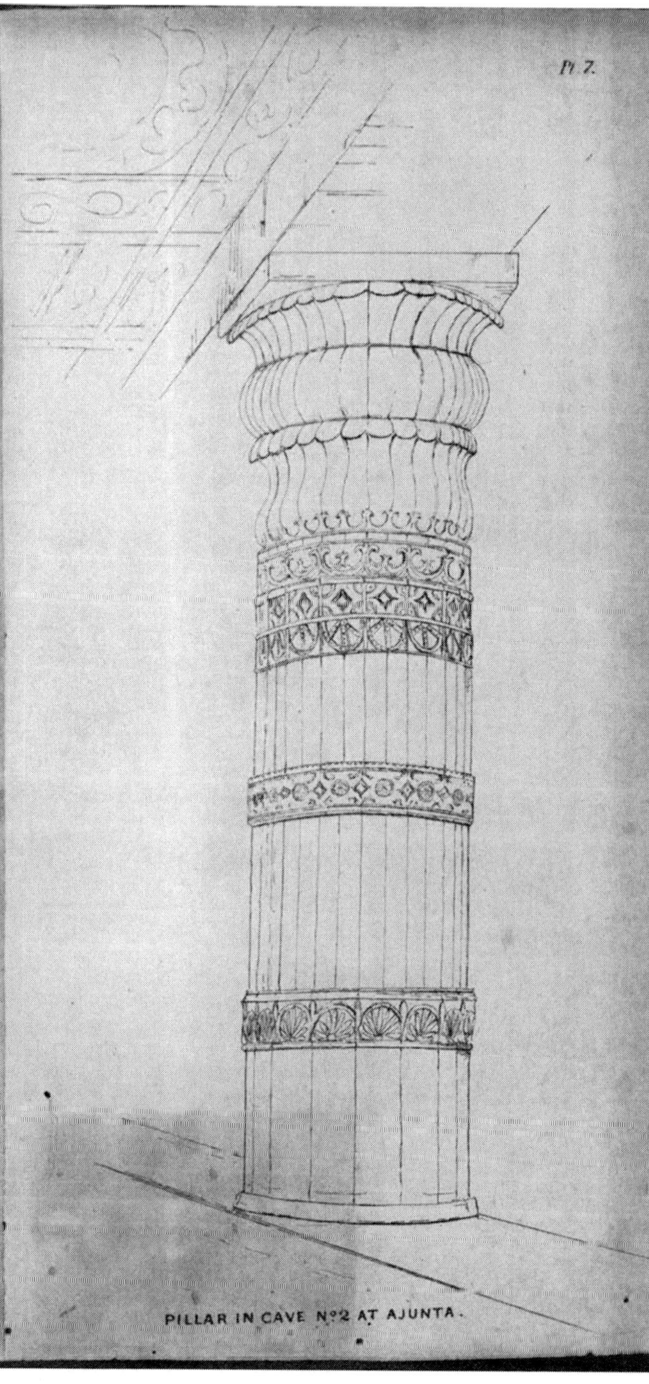

PILLAR IN CAVE No. 2 AT AJUNTA.

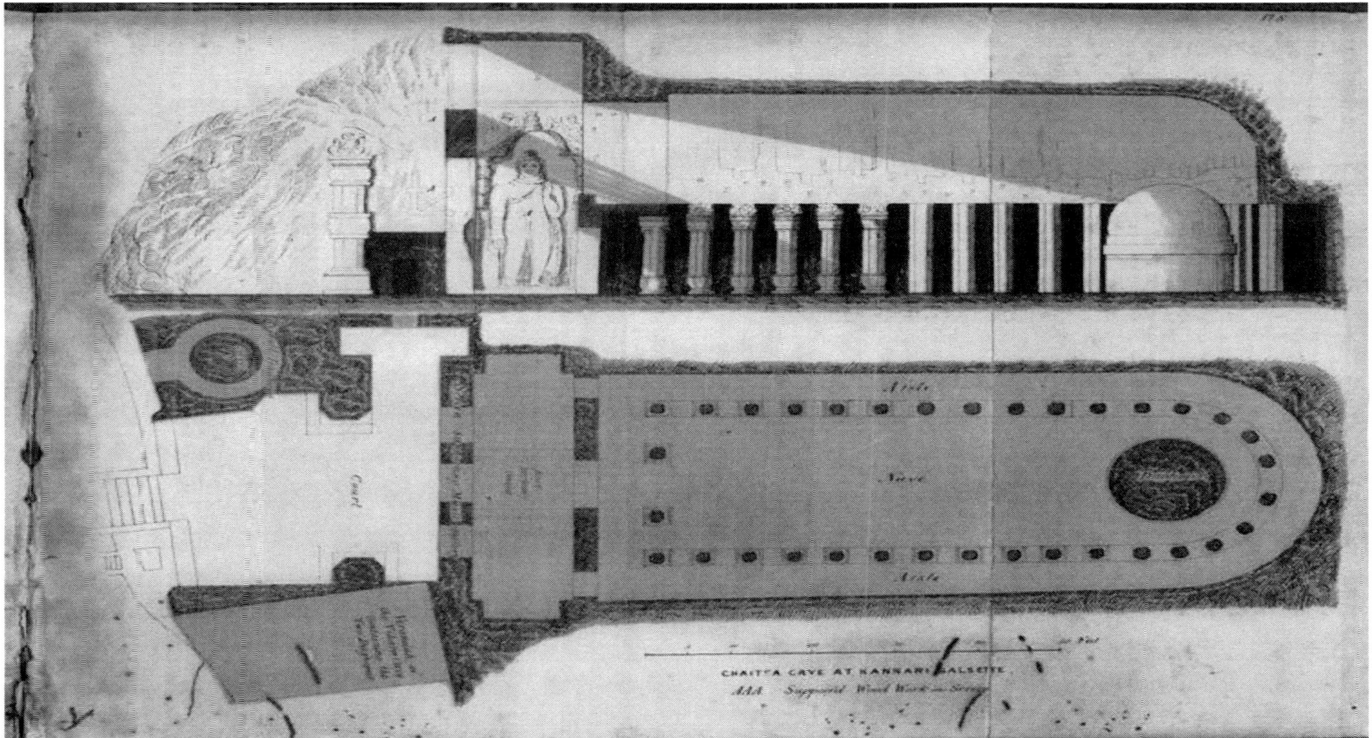
Aisle
Nave
Aisle
Court
CHAITYA CAVE AT KANHARI SALSETTE

PILLARS IN DOOMAR LENA, ELLORA.

Pl. 10.

PILLAR IN CAVE AT MAHAVELLIPORE.